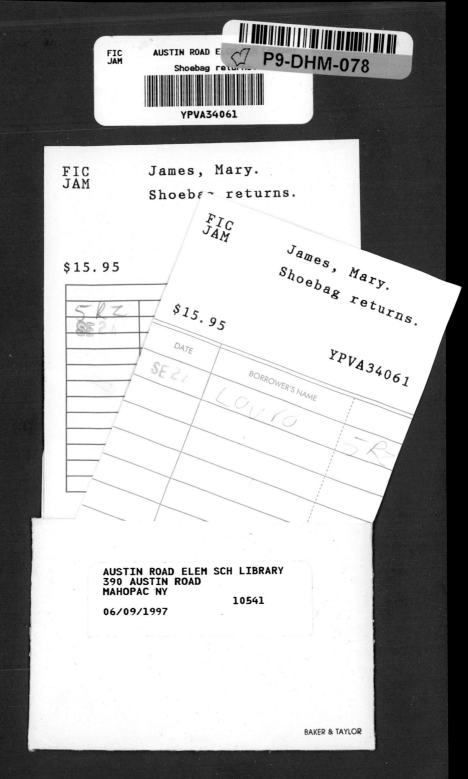

FIC
JAM

James, Mary.

Shoebag returns.

$15.95

FIC
JAM

James, Mary.

Shoebag returns.

$15.95

YPVA34061

DATE	BORROWER'S NAME	
SE 21	Laura	
		~R

Shoebag
RETURNS

Mary James

also known as M.E. Kerr

SCHOLASTIC PRESS / NEW YORK

Library of Congress Cataloging in Publication Data

James, Mary, 1927-
Shoebag returns / Mary James.
p.   cm.
Sequel to: Shoebag.

Summary: Shoebag, a cockroach with magical powers, changes himself into a
boy to aid lonely Stanley Sweetsong, the only boy in Miss Rattray's School for
Girls.
[1. Cockroaches — Fiction.   2. Schools — Fiction I.] Title.
PZ7.J1541She   1996   [Fic] — dc20   95-26123
CIP
AC

ISBN 0-590-48711-6

12 11 10 9 8 7 6 5 4 3 2 1   6 7 8 9/9 0 1/0

Printed in the U.S.A.   37

First Scholastic printing, November 1996

For Mary Rattray, walking companion on the trails of East Hampton and Montauk, New York, and in the Bas Languedoc, France . . . with thanks and love.

Shoebag
RETURNS

One

Like all cockroaches, Shoebag was named after his place of birth. It was the reason that wherever he was, he looked for a shoebag to snuggle into. The one he found this warm early autumn day was in the school dormitory. There were no shoes in it yet, for the students were just arriving by bus and car in the little village of Wayne, Pennsylvania.

Shoebag was having a strange dream. It was a dream of the magic time he'd become a little boy named Stuart Bagg. In the dream his cerci was missing, and so were his two back legs. So were his two middle legs, and so were his two front legs . . . and so were his antennae.

"I have tiny hands," he was crying out. "I have tiny feet! I have a tiny nose and tiny ears! I have a tiny head!"

"Wake *up*, Shoebag!" his mother shouted. "You are talking in your sleep!"

"I have become a tiny person," Shoebag continued.

1

"You have become nothing of the kind!" His mother flicked a front leg at his cerci, the cockroach name for a tail. A cerci is a remarkably sensitive structure, and even a light puff of air directed at a cerci can send a cockroach scurrying.

Shoebag sat bolt upright. "Where am I?" he said, wide awake now.

"You're right where you've been for two years," said Drainboard, his mother. "You're at Miss Rattray's School for Girls!"

"For girls," said Shoebag, "and now one boy."

"Yes. This year there will be one boy."

"That's why I was having the dream of when *I* was a boy."

"You were having a nightmare," Drainboard said, "even though it is only four o'clock in the afternoon."

"I was not afraid, though, Mama. So it was not a nightmare, was it?"

Drainboard said emphatically, "It was a nightmare! I remember all too well when you were a little boy. Your father and I lived in fear that you would step on us!"

"I could never step on you or my father, Under The Toaster, Mama. I was not that much of a person."

"But you needed three meals a day, Shoebag. You needed a bed and sheets and blankets! You needed clothes!"

"I needed soap and a washcloth," Shoebag said, remembering. "I needed money. I needed candy. I needed television."

"It *was* a nightmare!" Drainboard insisted. "You

2

just had a nightmare about the old days when we all lived in Brooklyn, New York."

"Those days weren't so bad, Mama."

"I remember happier ones, son, after you changed back to a roach."

"Like the times we had at the mall in Boston?"

"Exactly! Remember the dark closet behind the deli department, in that big store?"

"I remember."

"Home sweet home," said Drainboard.

"I would sneak down to Appliances to watch my old pal, Gregor Samsa, on television."

"Yes. Your little brother, Wheaties Box, was still alive then."

Shoebag smiled. "Remember what Gregor Samsa used to say, Mama?"

"I never watched television, son. You did."

"Gregor was the Great Breath spokesboy, Mama," said Shoebag. He scampered out of the shoebag, excited to remember Gregor. "He always said, 'Chew Great Breath!'"

"Gregor was a traitor to roachdom, son. He preferred being human to being one of us!"

"He couldn't help it, Mama. He wanted to be a star. A roach never gets to be a star."

"It is best not to look back," said Drainboard. "Live in the here and now, son. Here we are at Miss Rattray's School for Girls."

"And now one boy," Shoebag said.

"And now one boy," Drainboard agreed.

The roach family lived in the Lower School at Miss

Rattray's. It was more peaceful there, where the five-to-ten-year-olds boarded. Lights out at nine o'clock — not like the Upper School, where the racket of noisy young girls lasted right up until the ten o'clock news.

Another reason the roach family preferred to take up residence in the Lower School, was that it was nearer the kitchen.

Under The Toaster spent most of his time in there, foraging for snacks. He was the only member of the family not afraid of Cook's yellow cat, who always slept by the rag mop.

Drainboard said, "Stay awake now, son. We have to be on guard with all the students arriving today."

The moment she said that a noise no one *could* have slept through sounded. *WHACK! WHACK! WHACK!*

"Oh, no!" Shoebag said.

"Oh, *no!*" Drainboard moaned.

"The Doll Smasher is back!" both roaches said in unison, shuddering at the thought. "The Doll Smasher is back for another year!"

TWO

"Someday this will all be yours," said Mr. Sweet-song to his only son as the limo swept down the long drive leading from Castle Sweet. "But before you become the sole heir here, you must learn to be a gentleman and a scholar."

They were on their way to Miss Rattray's School for Girls (and now one boy).

"I'll learn to be a girl at Miss Rattray's, if you ask me," said Stanley.

"Miss Rattray's," said his mother, "was where I went to school, and where your grandmother went to school, and where your great-grandmother went to school. You should be honored to be accepted there."

"Where did *you* go, Father?" Stanley asked.

"I went to an ordinary school, son."

"There were no school songs at your father's school. No secret clubs, no school uniforms — they didn't even live in the school. They lived at home!"

"Well, it was an ordinary public school," said Mr. Sweetsong.

"A very, very ordinary public school. Be glad, Stanley, that you can be a Miss Rattray boy! The very first Miss Rattray boy there's ever been!"

But Stanley would miss Castle Sweet with its great gardens, its tiny red gazebo down by its round blue pond, and its long green lawns where Stanley played croquet with Tattle, the chauffeur. Often, after a game, Tattle would let Stanley see his pet tarantula, a South American red-toe called Weezer.

Stanley was ten years old, the very same age that his mother had been when she went to Miss Rattray's, and the very same age his father had been when he went to the very ordinary public school.

Stanley was short for his age, with brown hair and large brown eyes that fixed on Castle Sweet longingly as they left it. "I will miss my home," he said.

"But you will appreciate it more, dear, each time you return," said his mother.

"And when we see you next, at Thanksgiving," said his father, "you will already be bigger and braver than you are now, and you will probably be eager to go back to school."

"I am not brave," said Stanley, "and I will never be eager to leave Castle Sweet."

Behind glass, in the front seat, Tattle drove the limousine very slowly, for he knew Stanley wanted to prolong his last moments at the estate.

"I will miss Tattle, too," said Stanley, "and Weezer."

"Who ever heard of missing a chauffeur?" said his mother, "and who ever heard of missing a spider?"

"*I* would miss Tattle if he were to leave us," said Mr. Sweetsong.

"Who ever heard of a chauffeur leaving us?" said Mrs. Sweetsong. Cooks leave. Maids leave. Such servants come and go. But chauffeurs don't. Tattle loves our Rolls Royce."

"So do I," said Stanley.

"You are spoiled, darling," said his mother. "You probably think everyone lives as luxuriously as we do, but you will learn at Miss Rattray's that you are a very special little boy. Heir to a fortune!"

"If I'm a hair to a fortune, then —"

"Not *hair*, darling."

"Hair is what you have on your head, dear boy," said his father.

"If I'm an heir to a fortune, then why can't I keep my private tutor and not have to go away to school?"

"Because," said his mother, "you need friends."

"I don't know how to make friends."

"Besides," said his father, "we don't want you to be an heir with a big head. An heir with a big head would have too much hair to comb. Ha-ha."

"Not funny," said Stanley.

"Where does a sheep get his hair cut, son?" said his father.

"Where?" said Stanley.

"At the baa-baa shop. Ha-ha."

But nothing could make Stanley Sweetsong laugh late that afternoon in early September.

Tattle turned right at the end of the driveway and the long, silver limousine headed over the rolling hills of Bucks County, on the way to Wayne, near Philadelphia.

"What is Philadelphia known for, Stanley?" asked his mother, who was trying to get his mind off leaving home.

Stanley knew full well that it was the fourth largest city in the United States, known for Independence Hall, where the Declaration of Independence was signed. But he did not feel in a mood to mention independence when his own was being taken away. So he sat over in the corner of the backseat and sulked. And did not answer his mother.

"Here's a clue," said Mr. Sweetsong, "'. . . *and that government of the people, by the people, for the people, shall not perish from the earth.*'"

Mrs. Sweetsong said sharply, "That is the Gettysburg Address, dear. That is *not* the Declaration of Independence!"

"You see, Stanley?" said Mr. Sweetsong. "Your mother knows more than I do, because your mother went to Miss Rattray's School for Girls."

"And now one boy," said Mrs. Sweetsong.

Three

The lilting tones of Miss Rattray sounded down the hall.

"Your room," said she, "is right this way. . . .We are so pleased to have you, Stanley. Would you like some dinner? We are serving dinner in the dining hall."

"I'm not hungry, thank you, Miss Rattray."

"Well, then. You settle in and after dinner you'll meet the little girl who lives in the room next to yours."

"The Doll Smasher," Shoebag said. He stayed up in the corner of the ceiling, for he was known to be fairly fearless (except when he was expected to kill anything. And except around the yellow cat who lived by the rag mop in the kitchen).

Shoebag also wanted to get a good look at this boy, who was about to enter the very room where Shoebag had been sleeping earlier.

Miss Rattray led the small boy inside. "Your trunk is right there near the closet, Stanley. You may unpack it and put your clothes in the bureau drawers."

"At home a maid does that," said Stanley.

"But you are not home now, dear."

"Will I have a roommate, Miss Rattray?"

"On this particular hall, no one has roommates. You cannot have a roommate, for you are the only boy in Miss Rattray's School for Girls. And the little girl next door to you cannot have a roommate because —"

"Because," Shoebag silently finished the sentence for her, "she is a Doll Smasher."

"Because," Miss Rattray finished her own sentence, finally, "she is a very special little girl."

"So am I a very special little boy," said Stanley Sweetsong, "according to my mother."

"Then you two should get along very well, Stanley," said Miss Rattray. "You will share the bathroom across the hall."

Miss Rattray was a very tall, sturdy woman, who looked as though a string suspended from the ceiling was attached to her head. She had a very erect posture, large black spectacles, and short black hair. She wore a blue-and-white striped seersucker suit, for the school colors were royal blue and white.

"I hope you will be happy here, Stanley."

"The bed isn't made," said Stanley Sweetsong.

"Here we make our own beds, dear."

"I have never made my own bed in my entire life."

"No time like the present to start," said Miss Rattray.

10

Then with a smile and a wave she left the boy by himself in the room, except for Shoebag, now clinging to the twenty-second slat in the venetian blind.

When the boy sat down on the unmade bed, he put his hands up to his face and sobbed.

"Cheer up," Shoebag said. "It's not *that* bad here."

But, of course, humans rarely hear anything roaches have to say, and Stanley Sweetsong was crying too loud, anyway.

Four

W hy are you crying?" the little girl asked.
She was taller than Stanley, a skinny redhead
with freckles on her face, her arms, and probably on
her long legs, though Stanley could not tell for she
wore white knee socks. She was in the school uniform: a royal blue blazer with gold buttons, a white
shirt with a royal blue tie, and a white pleated skirt.

"I'm crying because I had to make my own bed and
unpack my own trunk, and I am also crying because I
am the only boy in Miss Rattray's School for Girls."

The little girl stood in the doorway, hands on her
hips, a look of exasperation on her freckled forehead.

"We cannot practice with you crying so loudly,"
she said.

"What do you practice?" Stanley asked.

"We are putting on a play, and the play must go
on!"

"No one told me anything about a play."

"My name," she said, "is Josephine Jiminez, and I am the director, producer, and playwright for the Black Mask Theater."

"My name is Stanley Sweetsong. I've been to theater, but it was in New York City. It was a play called *Cats*."

The little girl folded her arms and took one step into Stanley's room. "Our play is called *If You're Not In, You're Out!*"

Stanley said, "Can I see your play?"

"Do you have any Mallomars, Hydrox cookies, something like that? For dessert tonight we only got one awful pear."

"I have no food, just my allowance."

"How much do you get?"

"Five dollars a week."

"That's what it'll cost you to see it."

"But it is only Monday. What if I need money for the rest of the week? And what will I put in the offering in church, on Sunday?"

"You can't afford our play, I guess," she said.

"How long will it run? I could save up."

Josephine took another step forward. "It is the longest running play ever at Miss Rattray's School for Girls."

"And now one boy," said Stanley. "Where is this theater?"

"Right next door."

"In the next building?"

"In the next room," said Josephine.

"In a room like this room?"

"Not exactly like this room, since the Cast of Characters lives there with me."

"Then it must be a big, big room!"

"Come and see for yourself."

Stanley jumped down from the badly made bed, and followed the girl.

"Do the Cast of Characters share the bathroom across the hall with us?" he asked. He had never shared a bathroom with anyone. At Castle Sweet he had his own big bathroom.

"They don't need a bathroom," said Josephine.

"Everyone needs a bathroom."

"They *don't*!" she said. "You have to be quiet as we enter. They are in the middle of their rehearsal."

It was a dark room, for she had pulled the blinds shut. A floor lamp with its shade tilted was aimed at a square royal blue rug, filled with a dozen dolls.

"Shhhhh!" Josephine said.

On the bed, on the two chairs, on the bureau, there were more dolls.

All the dolls wore black masks.

Stanley had never seen so many dolls. He had never seen any doll wearing a black mask.

"All right, everybody!" Josephine shouted. "We'll have a ten-minute break!"

Stanley said, "So this is your theater."

"This is it," said the girl.

"And this is your Cast of Characters."

"This is it."

Stanley was too polite to say what he was thinking: that it was all just make-believe, that none of it was real.

14

"And what is your play about?" Stanley asked Josephine Jiminez.

"It's about a secret club."

"We belong to the Bucks County Country Club," said Stanley, "and also to the Red Fox Hunt Club."

"*Who* belongs to them?" Josephine asked as she moved two masked dolls aside to sit on the bed.

"We Sweetsongs do."

"But they are not secret clubs."

"No, they are not."

"And anyone can belong."

"No, they cannot. Only members can belong."

Josephine Jiminez heaved an impatient sigh and shook her head vigorously. "What I mean is, anyone can be a member."

"No, they cannot," Stanley insisted, "unless they have a lot of money."

"You cannot buy your way into *this* club!" said Josephine. "You don't know beans about this club. You don't know anything about such a secret club!"

"Why should I?" Stanley answered. "Where I come from clubs are not secret!"

"But you are here now," said Josephine. "And here there *is* one! And the one that there is, is the most important club in Miss Rattray's School for Girls . . . and now one boy."

"Then possibly I'll join it," said Stanley, looking around for someplace to sit where there wasn't a masked doll in the way.

"*Join* it?" said Josephine Jiminez, her eyes narrowing, her skinny body leaning forward. "JOIN IT?" she thundered. Then she let out a hoot of ridicule.

15

"I have to go back to my room," Stanley said, for he realized that he must have said something very laughable, or very sad, or very stupid . . . and possibly all three.

As he left the room, Josephine Jiminez was rocking back and forth on her bed filled with masked dolls, stamping her feet, holding tight to her freckled arms, laughing while she tried to exclaim:

"He thinks . . . he's . . . ha-ha . . . going to *join* the Better Club!"

Five

You had to be *asked* to be a member of the Better Club.

Even Under The Toaster had to laugh at the idea of anyone thinking he could join the Better Club, and Under The Toaster was not a big laugher.

Father of so many roaches he could not count them all, father of so many roaches he only remembered the ones who'd been felled by fatal accidents, when Under The Toaster *did* laugh, he roared.

No one in roachdom wanted him to laugh.

It was dangerous when he laughed.

On the rare occasions he was unable to keep from laughing, the yellow kitchen cat roused himself from his sleep and went on the prowl for any cockroaches scurrying around. This sent everyone scampering up walls and into floorboards.

Drainboard predicted that one day Under The Toaster would die laughing, or else he would be laughing while one of his own died.

Still, at their late-night picnic beside the hall night-light, Under The Toaster could not help himself.

"He thinks he can just join that club — har-de-har-har!"

And a moment after he'd roared at what Stanley Sweetsong had said, he blew a stale bread crumb at Shoebag's antennae and declared, "Even *you* were a smarter boy than that one, back when you were Stuart Bagg!"

"I was not a dumb boy, Papa."

But Under The Toaster could not forget, or forgive, that when Shoebag was a boy, he often saved teensy greasy morsels just for Drainboard. What kind of son broke the old roach rule that fathers *always* ate first and had their pick of choice treats?

So spitefully, Under The Toaster often teased his son about the time he'd changed into this tiny person.

"I remember when you were Stuart Bagg. You had to wear clothes!"

"I liked wearing them, Papa."

"But you couldn't wait to get back to being a roach!"

"It was not the clothes, though. It was because I missed you and Drainboard, and my brothers and sisters."

"Family is everything," said Under The Toaster. "I am head of the family so I am more than everything!"

"This is true, Papa," Shoebag agreed.

It was Gregor Samsa, a roach once himself, who had given Shoebag the formula to change back to a roach.

And it was Gregor Samsa who had gone back and forth from roach to human, before he decided to abandon roachdom for stardom.

Shoebag had never wanted to be a star. Besides missing his family, he had also missed having six legs, a shell, and antennae. He had missed the late-night picnics, like this one, too.

Still, there were times when he remembered sleeping in a bed, eating at a table, attending school — all the things he'd done when he was a tiny person. And Shoebag wondered at such times if it was possible for him to go back and forth just once more. Gregor Samsa had warned him never to do it without having a good reason.

Shoebag munched on the stale bread crumb his father had tossed his way and thought about it.

Down the hall, Josephine Jiminez was calling out, "Curtain Up!"

Shoebag had always enjoyed hanging out in Josephine Jiminez's little room with all the dolls. He liked to sleep there in the ear of a masked Kewpie doll named Monroe. The room was always nicely dark, too, for it was a theater. There were bits of food everywhere, as well, for Josephine Jiminez had a big appetite like Under The Toaster. She was always eating.

The catch (and there is always a catch when a roach finds a safe and agreeable place to dally) was the plays she put on in there.

"Curtain up!" she would call out, just as she had done a moment ago, and then the play would get underway.

19

The same old thing, time after time.

She made the Cast of Characters speak in various voices.

Monroe was the featured player, so Shoebag would have to hop out of the Kewpie doll's ear, and run off to the pencil sharpener on the wall.

The same old dialogue, time after time.

"You say you want to be a member of the club?" Monroe would ask in a deep and very stern voice.

Then Alexandria, the wooden doll with the rouged cheeks would answer, "Yes, please, can I get in?"

"You think you're good enough?" Monroe again.

"Yes, please, can I get in?" were the only lines Alexandria had, the only lines any of the bit players had.

Then Monroe would bark, "Well, you're *not* good enough!"

Next came the terrible moment when Josephine Jiminez reached out for the wooden doll.

And next came the vengeful voice which Josephine Jiminez gave to Monroe, shouting the lines:

"IF YOU'RE NOT IN, YOU'RE OUT!"

While Shoebag shivered inside the pencil sharpener, Josephine Jiminez would smash Alexandria against the wall.

WHACK! WHACK! WHACK!

"YOU ARE JUST NOT GOOD ENOUGH, ALEX-ANDRIA!"

They never were, were they?

The doll named Sam Houston wasn't. The doll named Arlington wasn't. The doll named Heidelberg wasn't. Nor was the doll named Seoul, the one named Washington, or the googly-eyed doll named Huntsville.

Just like Josephine Jiminez herself, not one doll in her collection was good enough to get into the club.

Not even Monroe was, really, for the play would always end with Monroe bellowing, "NONE OF US ARE GOOD ENOUGH! IF YOU'RE NOT IN, YOU'RE OUT!"

Even at that moment, the wall-whacking was in progress.

"What is that noise?" Drainboard asked.

"It's the Doll Smasher, that's all," Under The Toaster replied, his mouth full of half a pea.

"No, I mean that *other* noise," Drainboard said.

"What *is* it?" Under The Toaster said. "It's too low to be sobbing."

But it was not too low to be sobbing, when it was a small boy sobbing. Shoebag remembered that sound from his school days in Brooklyn when some little boys broke down and cried . . . and tried to hide it from big people and girls.

Shoebag had even made that sound once himself, when he was human, muffling it with a pillow.

Poor Stanley Sweetsong.

Shoebag's small roach heart went out to him, for Shoebag suddenly had a clear memory of his first night as a tiny person, naked, under bright lights in strange surroundings. . . . It was not always easy to be a little boy.

"Never mind. Eat up!" said Under The Toaster, and he pushed a wilted sprig of parsley at his wife, for he

21

was full, finally, and ready to crawl behind the light socket for a nap.

Shoebag would wait until his family was asleep.

Then he would crawl down to Stanley Sweetsong's room. Even if he could not make him feel better, he would be there for him. He would try to send him some cosmic cockroach message that would help him get through his misery.

Six

You could not miss a Better.

For one thing, a Better wore a white button with red letters which said WE'RE BETTER!

For another, a Better wore one red sock on the right foot, the regulation white one on the left.

Stanley Sweetsong noticed the Betters that morning in assembly. The Betters always had the better seats, down in the front row.

There were half a dozen of them there as everyone stood and sang the school song.

> *We are Miss Rattray's girls,*
> *We are Miss Rattray's pearls,*
> *Royal Blue to say we're true,*
> *White to show delight,*
> *At being in Miss Rattray's School,*
> *Hoo-rah, hoo-ray, We start our day*
> *Sing-ing,*

Sing-ing
Sing-ing!

After the assembly, Miss Rattray herself confronted Stanley Sweetsong as he started down the hall toward his first class.

"Why weren't you singing, Stanley Sweetsong?"

"I am not a girl. I could not sing that I am one, when I am the only boy."

"True," said Miss Rattray frowning, her head held high as always. Stanley stood next to her like a little bird towered over by a long-legged crane.

Stanley wore the royal blue blazer with the gold buttons, the white shirt, blue tie, and white pants.

"We will have to change the song," said Miss Rattray, "even though we have sung that song for one hundred and fifty years."

Just then a Better passed by and Miss Rattray caught her arm. "Patsy Southgate," she said, "please tell the Betters that we need a better song. . . . We need a song that includes Stanley Sweetsong here."

"Yes, ma'am," said Patsy Southgate, the only Better from the Lower School. "The Betters will write a better song."

"The Betters," said Miss Rattray to Stanley, "can do *anything*. That's why they're better."

"Could I ever be better?" Stanley asked her.

Both Miss Rattray and Patsy Southgate shook their heads doubtfully.

Both said, at the same time, "Oh, dear, I doubt that!"

This made Stanley Sweetsong very angry, for he had

never in his entire life been told it was doubtful he could be better.

He always thought he was the best.

He had always been told he was.

He had been told he was the best by his mother, by his father, by his tutor, and by Tattle, the chauffeur.

His first class that day was science.

"As you know," said Mr. Longo, "the Science Club is the only other club at Miss Rattray's."

Stanley raised his hand.

He said, "How would I know that?"

"Because I am telling you! There are only two clubs in this school. The Better Club and the Science Club."

"Can I *join* the Science Club?"

"You *may* if you win a prize. . . . Look up here at the two prizewinners from last year."

Mr. Longo had a mustache that drooped above his upper lip. He was bald, plump, and he carried a pointer.

He pointed at two tanks in the front of the room.

"In this one we have the snake," he said. "A king. . . . And in this one," he pointed to the second tank, "we have an African frog, who has buried himself in the mud."

"Why are they prizewinners?" Stanley asked.

"Because they have been captured, and put into environments similar to their own."

"Similar to their own?" Stanley said. "But the snake cannot unfurl, the tank is so small . . . and the frog has no sun, the way an African frog probably has."

Some of the girls giggled — not at Stanley's remark, though he didn't know that — but at the very idea of speaking up that way to Mr. Longo. No one ever answered Mr. Longo back.

Then a voice rang out, "Stanley's right!"

It was a familiar voice.

It was a familiar face at the back of the room, with familiar freckles and familiar red hair.

"If Stanley's right," Mr. Longo asked Josephine Jiminez, "what does that make me?"

"Wrong?" she asked.

Mr. Longo smiled so very sweetly, and he purred at the girl, "I beg your pardon, Josephine. Did I hear you say that I was wrong?"

"No, sir," she backed down. "I did not say you were. I asked if you were."

"Stanley Sweetsong, answer Josephine Jiminez. Am I wrong?" Mr. Longo's mustache quivered. His eyes were fixed like little black beads on Stanley's face.

A hush fell over the room.

"It looks that way to me," Stanley Sweetsong answered.

And Mr. Longo asked, "Do you know how your chances of ever getting into the Science Club look to *me*, Stanley Sweetsong?"

"Not very good?" Stanley suggested.

"Not good at all," Mr. Longo replied.

On my first day of school, Stanley wrote in his diary that night, *I did not do good at all, but at least I am not imprisoned in a tank. At least I have sunlight.*

Then while he was saying his prayers beside his bed ("Please, Lord, get me out of here!") he saw a small roach by his right knee and he reached for one of his Doc Martens to swat it.

Hand raised, the sole of the shoe ready to come down on the tiny critter, Stanley could not kill it.

"Just go *away*!" he told it.

He must have been very tired, and possibly only half-awake, for that was when the mind played tricks.

"If you want me to, I'll be your pal," he heard a voice say.

Now, it wasn't God's voice. It was too small and shaky to come from the Almighty, too much like Stanley's own voice when he'd prayed to the Lord to get him out of there!

And Stanley Sweetsong had never heard of such a thing as a talking roach. Even though there was not one single roach in residence at Castle Sweet, he knew none could speak.

"Who's there?" Stanley scrunched down and peered under his bed. Nothing there but some dust balls.

"My name is Stuart Bagg."

"Where are you, Stuart Bagg?"

"Hold your horses! First tell me if you need a pal."

"I do. I need one badly."

"Then you'll be seeing me," said the voice.

But he did not say when, or where he was, and he did not speak again that night.

Seven

ook hated one thing at Miss Rattray's School for Girls.

Cook hated the new computer.

It sat on a table right around the corner from the kitchen, near the Changing Room, which led into the swimming pool. It was a gift from the family of Josephine Jiminez.

Cook was a giant of a woman with frizzy yellow hair, the same color as the cat who slept by the rag mop. Both of them had green eyes, too. Though both of them had names, probably, no one called them by their names. The cook was Cook, and the cat was Cat.

This morning Cook was complaining about the computer to the only one within earshot: Cat.

"Ask me why I need a computer, and I will tell you I need a computer for the same reason a fish needs a bicycle. What am I to do with a computer?"

Now, Cat did not like questions. Questions woke

him up. Questions needed answers and Cat had none. Cat put a paw across his eyes and tried to get back to the dream he had of his other paw holding down a rat.

Cook was imitating the lilting tones of Miss Rattray when she had shown Cook the computer.

"Now you will be able to plan healthy meals, Cook, and keep track of when you served which one. Now you will have all your wonderful recipes right in front of you. Now you will know exactly how much fiber is in every meal, and how much protein, fat, and carbohydrates!"

Cook punctuated her imitation of the headmistress with a curse word.

The cat's tail swished angrily, for the cat could not bear profanity.

When Cook let loose more nasty words in a venomous tone which the cat had never before heard, the cat sat up.

He would have to give up his spot by the rag mop, and go elsewhere to rest.

It was then that the cat saw the roach.

The cat had seen him before, for he was a hungry pest, always foraging for food in the kitchen. Sometimes he was accompanied by his wife, who waited for him to toss her a few leftover crumbs.

Now, however, the roach was headed around the corner, to the room where the computer was.

"Ah! You see something!" Cook cried out. "What do you see, Cat?"

Cook watched the cat crouch down and slowly move away from the rag mop.

29

Then Cook saw what the cat saw.

"A cockroach! Eat him!"

But the roach was too fast. Out of the kitchen it went. Up one table leg it went. And into the computer.

"Good!" the cook said to the disappearing critter. "Go make a nest in there! Invite all your six-legged friends to join you! Have babies in there! Make yourself right at home!"

It was a hot autumn morning, and Cook was perspiring from the weather, her work at the stove, and her anger at the computer.

She struggled out of the T-shirt she was wearing over her sleeveless blouse. It was an old Hootie & The Blowfish T-shirt, a rock group whose music the cat did not enjoy. Mozart was more to the cat's taste: Bach, Beethoven.

Cook giggled as she put the T-shirt over the computer.

"I'll just cover it up!" she said. "Then I don't have to look at the thing!"

But the cat decided to keep looking at the computer, even though Hootie & The Blowfish stared back at him.

The cat believed that eventually the roach would reappear. Even though Cat was finicky about what he ate, as all cats are, he liked to bat roaches around. And Cat wouldn't mind having something real under his paw, instead of a rat in a dream.

Eight

After church, and before Sunday dinner, the students at Miss Rattray's were allowed to make phone calls.

"How is everything going?" Mrs. Sweetsong asked.

"Not great," Stanley said. "There are only two clubs here and it looks like I won't be asked to join either one."

"You already belong to the best clubs anywhere," said his mother. "The Bucks County Country Club and the Red Fox Hunt Club. They are the best clubs."

"There is one here that is better."

"Better than the best?" said Mr. Sweetsong, who was on one of the twelve extension phones at Castle Sweet. "There is no such thing as better than the best."

"There is, though, and they even have buttons that say WE'RE BETTER."

"Oh, dear, dear, dear," Mrs. Sweetsong sighed. "The Better Club. I had forgotten all about that wicked club! I once wanted to be a Better very, very badly, too!"

"Then how could you forget it?" Stanley asked.

"Time heals all wounds, dear. Often what was important long ago, is not even remembered later on."

Stanley said, "But it's not later on yet, for *me*. . . . And even if I could find some creature to collect for the Science Room, I would never get in *that* club. I told Mr. Longo he was wrong."

"Never tell a teacher he is wrong, even if he is," said Mrs. Sweetsong. "Teachers don't like to hear that they are wrong."

"I learned that," said Stanley sadly.

"Before I married your mother, I didn't belong to any club," said Mr. Sweetsong. "It didn't bother *me!*"

"It didn't bother you because there were no clubs in your school," said Stanley's mother.

"There was a Drama Club."

"That's not the same thing. Anyone could be in the Drama Club."

"I was not a club type, anyway," said Stanley's father. "I was not a snob until I married your mother."

"You are still not much of a snob," she said. Then she said, "But we didn't send Stanley off to school to be in clubs. We sent him there to learn to be a gentleman and a scholar . . . and to make friends."

"Do you have any friends?" asked his father.

Stanley decided not to say anything about the voice he had heard offering to be his pal. What had it said its name was? Something with "bag" in it. . . . Probably he had imagined it, anyway. Possibly being the only boy in an all-girl school was stressing him out.

He said, "I've made one friend named Josephine Jiminez."

She was standing just outside the phone booth, which was just outside the dining room. She had swiped a roll from a large tray being carried into the dining room by a waiter in a white coat.

Ever since they had sung "This Is the Feast of the Lord," in church, Josephine had begun to complain that she was hungry. . . . *Again*. . . . She was *always* hungry.

"Is she any relation to General Jiminez?" Mrs. Sweetsong asked.

"She is his daughter."

"Pedro Jiminez, hero of the Gulf War!" said Mr. Sweetsong.

"She calls herself an Army brat," said Stanley. He watched Josephine grab a butter ball from another passing tray.

Then the gong bonged for lunch: ONE TWO THREE.

Instantly Stanley heard the thunder of Miss Rattray's feet marching down the hall, *Plonk, Plonk, Plonk*. He saw the high-held head, the large black frame spectacles, the long and sturdy body. Behind her, children from the Lower School followed. Behind them, the Upper School girls.

And, of course, scattered among them were the Betters in their red and white socks, wearing their red and white buttons!

"I must go," Stanley shouted into the phone.

33

"Good-bye, sweetie!" his mother said. "Remember, time *does* really heal all wounds."

"And time flies very fast," said his father, "because so many people are trying to kill it! . . . Good-bye, son!"

Stanley called to Josephine Jiminez, "Look out! Hide the roll! Hide the butter!"

Josephine thrust the roll into the pocket of her blazer with one hand, the other held the butter.

"Happy Sunday morning, Josephine," Miss Rattray called out. Patsy Southgate, the Lower School Better, trailed behind her, pulling up her one red sock, looking smug, ignoring Josephine and Stanley. The Betters could look right through you, Stanley thought to himself. Nobody had attitude like a Better.

Miss Rattray stuck out one of her large hands as she approached Josephine. Quickly, Josephine slipped the butter ball to Stanley.

"Happy Sunday morning," Josephine sang out and shook the outstretched hand.

Miss Rattray let go of Josephine's hand, noticed something on her own hand, but carried on bravely with a handshake for Stanley. "Happy Sunday morning, Stanley."

"Happy Sunday morning," he answered, feeling her large fingers squash the ball of butter.

"What . . . on . . . earth?" Miss Rattray pulled her buttered hand back and stared down at it. "What . . . is *this!*"

"Butter," Josephine said. And then she giggled. "We're butter."

But it was not a joke Miss Rattray appreciated. Her

face was dour. Her sticky hands fluttered as the Betters pulled Kleenex from their pockets to offer to her.

"You two are grounded," Miss Rattray told Josephine and Stanley, "until further notice. Immediately after you finish eating, go to your rooms!"

Nine

D oes your smile smell?" a young boy on television asked. He wore dark glasses, and his teeth were very white.

Everyone in the recreation room of the Lower School shouted back at him.

"NO! DOES YOURS?"

Then there were silly giggles from the small viewers, gathered around the TV. This was their favorite commercial.

Sunday was the only day they could watch television, and only for two hours after Sunday dinner.

"Chew Great Breath!" said their beloved TV spokesboy, while dancing packages of gum circled around him humming the Great Breath song.

Why should your smile smell like death?
Why should you wake up with bad breath?
Chew chew chew and you'll get through
Chew chew chew, Chew Great Breath!

"YOU CHEW IT!" everyone shouted. "*WE* CAN'T *CHEW* GUM!"

Shoebag could not believe his eyes, or his luck.

Chased by the yellow cat from the kitchen to the recreation room, he thought he was a goner until he leaped up on the piano, and slid in between a black key and a white one. While one girl grabbed the cat to hug, another shushed everyone so they could hear (of all people!) Gregor Samsa!

Shoebag's antennae bristled with joy.

There was his old friend and ex-roach, the very one who had come to Shoebag's rescue so many times back when Shoebag was that tiny person named Stuart Bagg.

Shoebag remembered playing in a park, swinging in a swing, having his own pencil box, a pair of brown boots, a blue wool scarf. Oh, he *had* liked wearing clothes!

When Stuart Bagg had needed a pal, Gregor Samsa had been there for him. . . . And now, shouldn't Shoebag be there for Stanley Sweetsong? Hadn't he already promised to be his pal? Wasn't that a good reason to go forth?

Shoebag could have been a smudge on the sole of a Doc Marten, if Stanley Sweetsong had not taken pity on him.

Now Stanley Sweetsong was off in his room, grounded by Miss Rattray, with only the Doll Smasher for company.

"Gregor Samsa!" Miss Rattray's girls were shrieking so loudly the yellow cat fled, tail between its legs.

Shoebag felt that old tingle under his shell as he remembered the formula for change, which Gregor had told him to say.

The timing was perfect, too, for Drainboard, Under The Toaster, and Shoebag's two brothers, Radio and Garbage Pail, had moved into the computer down by the kitchen.

Shoebag doubted that Cook had ever invited them to live there, though Under The Toaster swore she had.

Shoebag did not want to live inside a Macintosh, no matter how dark and safe it was, for Shoebag thrived on action and the sounds of people.

He would have to wait for Wednesday night, when the formula worked best.

Meanwhile, he would try to remember all the things he would need to know when he went forth changed to a tiny person.

He would need to know how to walk upright again and how to go down slides. How to swing and how to play computer games. How to lick an ice-cream cone and how to avoid bullies. How to eat those wiggling white worms called spaghetti.

Possibly, he would need a television schedule, too.

Ten

The Black Mask Theater was darkened for this Sunday matinee.

The Cast of Characters did not usually perform on Sunday, but Stanley and Josephine were not allowed to watch TV in the Recreation Room.

"All because of a butter ball!" Josephine grumbled.

"It was not the butter ball that made Miss Rattray angry," Stanley said. "It was making fun of the Better Club. You never should have said, 'We're Butter.'"

"Do you want to see *If You're Not In, You're Out,* or don't you?" Josephine asked him. "It's your opportunity to get in for nothing."

"It's gloomy in here," said Stanley. "I would rather let some light in. It's such a nice day out!"

"But we're *in!*"

"We're in, all right. We're in trouble, too."

"Miss Rattray will get over it. She always forgives, particularly on Sundays. Hand me Monroe, the Kewpie doll. The curtain is about to go up."

39

"Do you know what they call you, Josephine? They call you the Doll Smasher."

"Because they are jealous."

"What I heard is that *you* are jealous. Jealous of the Betters."

"I don't smash the Betters' heads in my play. I smash the heads of the dolls who aren't good enough to get in the club."

"So I heard," said Stanley. "And none of them are good enough!"

"Then how could I be jealous?"

"*I'm* jealous," Stanley admitted. "I am not used to being told I cannot be in a club."

"Get used to it!" Josephine said. "Curtain going up."

But Stanley had heard all about her play, and now he was not eager to see it. He did not think he would enjoy a play in which dolls were whacked against the wall. He did not like the darkened room, and the black masks across the dolls' eyes.

"Why do they have to wear those masks?" he asked.

"Because it is the Black Mask Theater. You have to be dramatic if you're in theater. You have to be mysterious. Theater is supposed to be magical."

Stanley said, "If you smash the dolls against the wall because they can't get into the secret club, isn't it like smashing your own head against the wall because you can't be a Better?"

"Now you talk like the shrink who visits this school on Fridays."

"Does he visit *you*?"

"I visit *him*. 'Josephine,' he says, 'why are you so angry?'"

"What do you say?"

"I say I'm an Army brat, and we're all angry because our fathers go to wars!"

"But your play isn't about fathers going to wars."

"I say I'm hungry all the time, and hungry people are all angry!"

"But your play isn't about hunger."

"I say who cares about the clubs in this school, anyway? I'm not angry about any stupid clubs!"

"But your play," Stanley persisted, "is about a stupid club."

"Curtain going up!" said Josephine.

"Meow!"

"No catcalls, or you have to leave!" said Josephine.

"I didn't meow," Stanley said.

"Someone did," said Josephine.

"Meow!"

The large yellow cat with slanted green eyes walked toward the royal blue rug, and sat down in the spotlight beside the googly-eyed doll, Huntsville.

"How did *he* get here?" Josephine said.

"A cat! I've always wanted a cat!" Stanley said. He jumped off the bed, went across, and knelt down by him.

"If you always wanted one, how come you never had one?"

"They ruin good furniture my mother says, and my father says they get hair all over good clothes."

The cat squeezed his eyes shut in ecstasy as Stanley petted him.

"Clear the stage!" said Josephine. But she could not resist the cat, either. (She could not resist any animal,

41

any bug, any creature great or small.) She knelt down beside Stanley and petted the cat, as well.

"Do you want to be in a play?" she asked the cat.

"You'd better not smash *his* head against the wall."

"I wouldn't," she said. "I hate all cruelty. That's why I said you were right in Mr. Longo's class."

"You took it back," Stanley said.

"I didn't take it back. I just wormed my way out of it. Nice kitty. Nice kitty."

"A yellow cat!" Stanley said. "I've never seen a yellow cat! Only white ones, or black ones, or Siamese."

"We should name him Butter," Josephine said. "He's the color of butter, and that butter ball is what got us grounded."

"Hello, Butter," Stanley said to the cat. "Where do you live?"

"I think he belongs to Cook," said Josephine. "They say the kitchen has rats!"

"Rats in the kitchen!" Stanley said. "How can we eat the food?"

"They're not in the food. They're just in the kitchen."

"There are no rats at Castle Sweet!"

"But you're not at Castle Sweet now," said Josephine. "You're in this cruel boarding school where the Betters strut around in their red socks wearing their Better buttons."

"I saw a roach in my room, too," said Stanley. He said nothing about the voice he heard after he saw the roach.

"Roaches don't bother me," said Josephine Jiminez. She leaned over and nuzzled the yellow cat. "I would rather have them around than certain people and their secret club! Everything I need is right in this room. The Black Mask Theater, the Cast of Characters, you and me, and now Butter! Who cares about anything else?"

But her voice had a very needy sound. And Stanley Sweetsong was thinking that there he was in a dark room on a sunny day with a ditzy girl everyone called the "Doll Smasher." At Castle Sweet he would have been out on the great green lawn with a croquet mallet, batting balls through the wicket.

Eleven

It was late on a Wednesday night, pitch-dark except for a slice of orange moon.

Inside the Macintosh, all the roaches were fast asleep but one.

He was perched at the door of the disc drive, listening for any sound besides the hum of the refrigerator in the kitchen, and the water filter in the swimming pool.

Then Shoebag hopped down to the keyboard.

He drew a deep breath, let it out, and spoke the roach formula Gregor Samsa had taught him.

"Flit, flutter, quiver, quaver, totter, stagger, tumble, warble, wobble, wiggle, swing, and sway."

You would think that when a roach turned into a tiny person there would be a sound of some kind, a pop or a snap, or a poof with a puff of smoke.

But there was none of that.

As soon as Shoebag said the words he felt his shell lift, his legs dissolve, his cerci vanish, and his antennae float off.

His two human eyes saw himself become, quite soundlessly, a small, very naked, young boy.

Instantly, he covered his private parts with his small hands, then whispered "Oh dear, oh dear, I forgot about clothes."

But right in front of him, covering the computer, was an old Hootie & The Blowfish T-shirt.

Stuart Bagg lifted it up carefully, for he did not wish to disturb the sleep of his roach family — a very deep sleep, since they had feasted on an extra-large late-night picnic, filled with crunchy morsels. Shoebag had spent days gathering them, so their dear roach bodies would be exhausted from gobbling the crumbs down.

The T-shirt was way long, past his knees, the short sleeves past his elbows.

He was barefoot, of course, and his hair was uncombed.

The cat appeared as he stood there, and wound himself in and out between his legs, nipping his ankles.

Sometimes cats were suspicious of small boys who'd once been roaches. Stuart Bagg knew that from experience. Sometimes cats batted at your feet as though you were still an insect, and sometimes they followed you.

This cat was no exception.

"Scat!" said Shoebag. "Please scat!"

The cat jumped away, but he sat at the door to the kitchen eyeing Shoebag thoughtfully.

Then, while everyone in the school was still asleep, Stuart Bagg set off to find some shoes.

Twelve

O h, no you don't!" said Stanley Sweetsong, leaping out of his bed.

"I thought you were asleep!" said Stuart Bagg. He dropped the boy's Doc Martens on the floor.

"Stay right where you are!" Stanley said.

"Where would I go without shoes or pants?" Stuart Bagg asked him.

In his blue-and-white striped pajamas, Stanley padded over to the light switch and pressed it.

Then he stood with his hands on his hips, glaring at Bagg, muttering "Thief! You are a thief in the night!"

"I am Stuart Bagg, Stanley. Remember when you said you needed a pal? I am your pal."

"What kind of a pal steals my only pair of Doc Martens?"

"You have many pairs of shoes, and I have none, Stanley."

The two boys were the same height, and the same

weight. While Stanley Sweetsong had brown eyes and brown hair, Bagg's hair was red, his eyes were blue, and his face was full of freckles.

"This is a trick," said Stanley, "and I think Josephine Jiminez is in on it. You have red hair and so does she. You have freckles and so does she. Maybe you are her brother."

This was the hardest part about changing from a roach to a boy, explaining it.

It would never do for Stuart Bagg to say that only moments ago he had been a cockroach.

He could never tell anyone from whence he came. Humans were too logical and practical to accept the truth. Humans were too finicky to be chums with ex-cockroaches.

"Josephine Jiminez is not my sister," said Stuart Bagg. "She is not a part of this, and you must never tell her about me."

"Who can I tell about you then? She is my only friend."

"You must not tell anyone, Stanley."

"But where did you come from?"

Stuart Bagg remembered what Gregor Samsa used to say. " 'I come from here and there. I go back and forth.' Don't you remember the night you were saying your prayers, and I told you I'd be seeing you?"

Stanley Sweetsong sat down on his bed. He shook his head and rubbed his eyes, then opened them again as though he expected Bagg to be gone. "I was having a horrible nightmare of being put into a tank in the Science Room," he said. "I have you to thank for waking me up, but maybe I am not awake at all. Or maybe I am awake but seeing things that aren't there!"

"You are seeing me, and I am here. You'll see me as long as you need a pal. Then *pffft* — I'll disappear."

"Not in my Doc Martens, though."

"Not if you say not. I only wanted to be better dressed when we first met. I wanted to make a good impression."

Stanley Sweetsong looked chagrined. "I have a lot of clothes," he said "and you *are* the same size I am."

"I won't wear anything of yours you really care about."

"You can wear whatever you want to wear," said Stanley Sweetsong. "Clothes will get you nowhere in Miss Rattray's School for Girls, and now *two* boys."

"One boy. I am not enrolled here."

"You are lucky then. This is a cruel school. There are helpless animals imprisoned in the Science Room. There are secret clubs, too, which you cannot join!"

"Once," said Stuart Bagg, "I attended a school where not everyone was bright and beautiful, so we had a club for the rest of us."

"If you want to, you can wear my Doc Martens," Stanley said. "Shoes won't get you anywhere in this place, either!"

"We sang a song," Bagg continued. "It began 'Here's to the rest of us. Here's to the best of us. . . . Here's to our power. Here's to —'"

Stanley Sweetsong interrupted. "No one has any power in this place but Miss Rattray, the Betters, and the members of the Science Club. No one ever will, either!"

"Because no one has ever tried to start a third club!" Stuart Bagg sat down in the chair opposite Stanley and rubbed his feet. Feet took some getting used to. Bagg wiggled his toes. His toes were bigger than any of the members of his family. Feet and toes were an insect's enemies, particularly when they were in shoes. For sure, when they were in Doc Martens.

"Why not start your own club?" Bagg said. He looked across at the mirror over Stanley's desk. He saw Stanley, a round-faced, pensive boy with brown hair and brown eyes. And then he saw his true self: a cockroach with its antennae pointing. For once a roach, always a roach: The mirror never lied, even though he *had* become a tiny person.

"A club is a hard thing to start," said Stanley Sweetsong. "A club needs members."

"A club needs a name, too," Bagg said.

"A club could use a mascot like Butter the cat!"

Butter had always been Shoebag's very favorite food. Bagg almost drooled at the thought of it.

"We can be the Butter Club! Just like Josephine said: We're Butter!"

And then and there the Butter Club came into being.

Bagg helped Stanley make Butter Club badges, and he also helped Stanley make his bed, for he stayed in Stanley's room until the sun came up, and the first bell rang.

"I have to go now, Stanley."

"Go where, Bagg?"

"Don't worry. I will come back. I promise."

"You'd better. You have my clothes, remember, and you are my pal, remember."

"I'll remember," Bagg said.

Thirteen

We are Miss Rattray's girls, and boy
We are Miss Rattray's girls, ahoy!
Royal blue to say we're true,
White to show delight,
At being in Miss Rattray's School,
Hoo-rah, hoo-ray, We start our day
Sing-ing,
Sing-ing,
Sing-ing.

Josephine dug her elbow into Stanley's side and whispered out of the side of her mouth, "*Ahoy?* We are not at sea, are we? When did we become sailors?"

"Blame Patsy Southgate," Stanley whispered back. "She wrote it."

Miss Rattray stood at the podium peering out at them through her black spectacles. "Before you leave to attend your classes," she said, "I have one announcement! There are rumors that the cook's cat has been seen in the upstairs of the Lower School. Animals are not allowed, as you know very well! Anyone found harboring an animal will lose her, or *his* privileges."

"Ahoy," said Josephine under her breath. "What privileges are those? The privilege of being locked away in a boarding school? The privilege of going hungry because all the portions of food in the dining room are not enough to keep the kitchen rats alive? The privilege of being kept out of the school clubs?"

"Not *all* the school clubs," Stanley said. "Not anymore. Are you ready to spring our surprise on everyone?"

"Ready, mate," Josephine gave him a snappy salute.

Both had on one yellow sock. Both wore their cardboard buttons painted yellow, reading WE'RE BUTTER!

The first one to notice, and comment, was of course, the president of the Better Club, C. Cynthia Ann Flower.

"How very sorry you're going to be, Stanley and Josephine," she said. "How very sorry I am that I have to report this immediately!"

When anyone was very rich, Stanley's mother always said the person was rich rich. And if anyone was very dirty, Stanley's mother always said the person was dirty dirty. Stanley's mother would have called C. Cynthia Ann Flower beautiful beautiful. She was known for it. Known for her long, black, shiny hair that fell halfway down her back. Known for her sky-blue eyes and rosy complexion. Known for her play clothes from Banana Republic and Saks Fifth Avenue. Known for her VCR tapes of every commercial starring Gregor Samsa, plus one of every sitcom in which he had a minor part. Known to have her school blazer and skirt tailor-made. Known to be rich rich and snobbish snobbish.

She was an Upper School pupil, thirteen years old, and fluent in French.

Often, in times of crisis, she slipped into that language, as she did that Monday morning.

"*Mon Dieu!*" she said. "What could you two be thinking of, to pull such a *stupide* stunt?"

Off she strutted in the direction of Miss Rattray's office.

Several other Betters looked down their noses as they passed Josephine and Stanley in the hall.

But Ethel Lampert, a mousy young Lower School girl, stopped them. She was known for her stamp collection and little else.

"What is this Butter Club all about?" she asked them.

"Mostly, it's about not getting into the other two clubs," said Stanley.

Josephine gave him the elbow again and whispered, "Don't make us look like losers. We have to have style. We have to buy a box of Butterfingers at the school store, and present one to each new member. That will give us a little flair. And we can never be easy to get."

"If you ever become easy to get," said Ethel Lampert, who had overheard Josephine, "will you let me know?"

"We vote you in," said Stanley confidently.

"We do?" Josephine gave him a look. "I don't even have the Butterfingers yet!"

"We have to have founding members. I remember that from the Red Fox Hunt Club, where my father is a founding member."

"All right, welcome to the Butter Club," Josephine told her. "Come to my room after classes for a Butterfinger. But you have to stop with the stamps. We don't want any stamp collectors. They're too lonely."

"I won't be lonely now," Ethel Lampert said.

"Get yourself a yellow sock," said Josephine. "I'll make up a button for you . . . and, Ethel?"

"Yes, Josephine? What is it?" Ethel's voice was tinkling with joy, her face alight with surprise and wonder.

"Don't tell anyone how easily you got in."

"Oh, I won't," said Ethel, who would.

How could she keep such an unexpected honor to herself?

Pleased with themselves, never mind that they had taken in a less than dynamic girl as their first member, the Butters went skipping down the hall to science class.

There, their moods soon changed.

Mr. Longo waited until everyone was seated to reveal his own new acquisition.

His drooping mustache wiggled as he tried to contain a triumphant smile. He wanted absolute silence before he pulled the black silk cloth away from the third tank.

"What have we here, I wonder," he trilled in a teasing tone. "What has Mr. Longo got to show you?"

Josephine whispered to Stanley, "Another poor critter."

"Another object of torture," Stanley agreed.

"Thanks to C. Cynthia Ann Flower, who I am now appointing president of the Science Club, we have a new prize specimen she ordered from a catalog!" said Mr. Longo.

"But C. Cynthia Ann Flower is president of the Betters!" Josephine wailed.

"Now she is president of both clubs," Mr. Longo responded.

"But prizewinners are supposed to catch their own specimens," Josephine wailed again. "Not order them from a catalog."

"Prizewinners can do as they please, which is why they are prizewinners," said Mr. Longo. "And here we have the biggest, the hairiest, and the very scariest spider you have ever seen!"

With a fast turn of his hand he swept away the silk cover.

"A *Sericopelma communis!*" he announced, rubbing his fat fingers together gleefully. "A tarantula!"

Fourteen

Just because you live inside a Macintosh, does not mean you do not know what is going on outside one.

Word of the new tarantula had spread very fast, and Under The Toaster's family was talking of little else that morning.

"Shoebag, Shoebag! You're alive!" Drainboard cried out when Shoebag slipped through the disc drive.

"Of course I'm alive, Mama! Why wouldn't I be?"

"Because there's a tarantula in the Science Room!" she said. "What spider wouldn't *kill* for the taste of you, Shoebag? So when you didn't come home all night, we thought you'd been found and fed to that hairy arachnid!"

"We even said 'Go to a better life,'" Radio told his brother, "the Cockroach Prayer for the Dead."

"Well, I am alive and well," Shoebag told them all. "I was only away overnight."

Of course he could not tell them where he'd been, or what he'd been while he was there. They would only scold him, and nag him to tell them the formula for becoming a tiny person. If he ever told the formula, it would lose its power for him forever. When Gregor Samsa had given it to Shoebag, he had given up his ability to go back and forth.

So Shoebag tried to make light of his absence, even though Under The Toaster was not speaking to him now.

"Tell my son," he said to Drainboard, "about the missing T-shirt, too, the one with Hootie & The Blowfish on it!"

Shoebag had left it in Stanley's room when he had put on Stanley's jeans, one of his Polo shirts, and his Doc Martens. Those clothes were just around the corner in the Changing Room, where students changed into swimming suits before they used the pool. Where else but in the Changing Room would Stuart Bagg become Shoebag again?

Drainboard said, "The T-shirt Cook put over our Macintosh has disappeared. She is looking everywhere for it. Papa says it's a bad omen."

"Tell my son," said Under The Toaster, "that someone is eyeing our Macintosh, and it isn't the cook!"

"Tell Papa not to worry," Shoebag said.

"Tell him we have lost our cover!" said Under The Toaster, "and it is a bad omen!"

"Do not stray again, Shoebag," said Drainboard. "We may have to move someplace new in a hurry, and we do not want to move without you."

"I'll find you, Mama. Don't worry," said Shoebag.

"DON'T YOU *MAKE* US WORRY!" Under The Toaster thundered finally speaking directly to his son. "Things are changing around this place. A tarantula comes, a T-shirt goes. It's a bad omen!"

"Stick close to the computer, son," Drainboard said.

"You are foolhardy and reckless!" said Under The Toaster, "and you are asking for trouble!"

But Shoebag had promised Stanley Sweetsong he would return.

He played a few roach games with Radio and Garbage Pail, and found a bit of salami in the kitchen for Drainboard, and her favorite snack: rye bread crumbs.

"Aren't you hungry?" Drainboard asked. "Out all night and half the morning? Don't you want to eat this?"

Shoebag had no time to answer, for Under The Toaster snatched the food. "I eat first and best!"

"They are for Mama!"

"Let Papa have them, dear," Drainboard said what she always said. "Papa's been so worried you were given to the tarantula to eat."

And so it went, until all creatures in the Macintosh were ready for their afternoon nap . . . all but Shoebag.

Off to the Changing Room he went.

Then: "Flit, flutter, quiver, quaver, totter, stagger, tumble, warble, wobble, wiggle, swing, and sway."

Stuart Bagg reached behind him for the clothes he had borrowed from Stanley.

They were gone!

"EEEEEEEEEEK!" from the mouth of a little girl, on her way to her diving lesson. "EEEEEEK! A naked boy!"

Fifteen

Stanley Sweetsong, you have some explaining to do!"

Stanley sat up on his bed, eyes as wide as Miss Rattray's were narrow behind her black frame glasses. Head held high, back stiff, she said, "Are you going to invite me to sit down?"

"Sit down," said Stanley, and she did, ramrod straight in the chair beside his bed. In her hands she held a small pile of clothing: Levi's, a Polo shirt, and Doc Martens.

"This afternoon," she said, "I found these in the Changing Room. Your name tag is on them."

"I don't know how they got there," said Stanley, who knew the only one who could have left them there was Bagg.

"About an hour ago, little Lucy Lightite saw a naked boy fleeing from that very room."

"I've been right here ever since classes ended, ma'am."

"You are up to something, Sweetsong!" said Miss Rattray, who only called students by their last names when she was furious. "And I think I know what you are up to!"

"What am I up to, ma'am?"

"I think you want to be sent home."

"I just got here, ma'am."

"I know you just got here! But you are doing things to test my patience, Sweetsong. There is something else I have on my mind, too. You know that we have only two clubs here."

"Yes, ma'am."

"And that is all we have ever had here. Now, I see that many of the Lower School girls believe they, too, can become —" Miss Rattray had a bit of trouble getting out the word, "Butters."

Stanley said nothing, for what was there to say?

Miss Rattray said, "I had to shoo away a line of girls from Josephine Jiminez's door as I came down the hall."

"Yes, ma'am," Stanley agreed, for he had seen the line himself. He had wondered why suddenly Josephine Jiminez had become popular, since she never was before. Neither did she ever let other girls into the Black Mask Theater.

So it was Ethel Lampert who had brought this about! Ethel Lampert, who broke her promise, and spread the word how easily she had become a founding member of the Butters! Now everyone but a Better wanted to be a Butter! Everyone but a Better wanted a Butterfinger!

Miss Rattray said "It is one thing for poor, thin, angry Josephine to be part instigator in this undertaking. For poor, thin, angry Josephine is under the care of the school psychologist who visits us on Fridays. She has not had an easy life being a child of the military, her family moving about constantly, her dolls her only company. But *you*, Sweetsong, have had a very lovely life so far."

"Yes, I have," Stanley agreed, and did not wonder aloud why it ever had to stop so he could attend a girls' boarding school.

If it was not for Bagg, Josephine Jiminez would not be the only one who needed to see the school psychologist.

If it was not for Bagg, Stanley might never have awakened from the nightmare, would never have thought up the Butter Club, nor made the yellow Butter badges. Bagg had even helped him make his bed! That was a *real* pal!

They had done a sloppy job on the bed. Stanley took this opportunity to turn back the top sheet as he sat there.

"You're not such a good bed maker, either, are you?" said Miss Rattray.

"I have never had to make my own bed."

"So you said the first day we met, Stanley."

"So I said."

"But a bad bed maker is one thing, and a bad sport is another."

"I don't like sports at all," said Stanley, "except for croquet, which I play with Tattle on the great, green lawns at Castle Sweet."

"*Played*," said Miss Rattray firmly. "You are not *at*

Castle Sweet now. You are here." She crossed her long legs and pushed her black-framed spectacles back on her nose. "What I mean by a bad sport is someone who turns bitter at the fortune of others, just as you were bitter over the Betters, and formed the Butters."

Miss Rattray's point was punctuated then by a *WHACK! WHACK! WHACK!* against the wall next door.

It seemed the Black Mask Theater was having a surprise matinee, though that was not the custom at all.

"Speaking of bad sports," Miss Rattray sniffed, "Josephine Jiminez seems to be acting out her rage once again. No wonder she is called the Doll Smasher!"

"Maybe she is mad because you sent away the line of girls in the hall. No one has ever lined up to see her before!"

WHACK! WHACK! WHACK!

Butter, the cat, must have been on his way into the Black Mask Theater when the whacking began, then changed his mind. For suddenly out of the corner of one eye, Stanley saw the creature dart through the door of his room, and disappear under his bed.

Miss Rattray held her head so very high, she never saw Butter. If she had, Stanley would have been in more trouble, for cats were not allowed anywhere but the kitchen.

"Why," she asked, "does the Better Club bother you?"

"It bothers me that I'm not in it," Stanley said.

"But all through life there will be some clubs you will not be in. That is just a fact of life, dear boy."

"That is why I started my own club," said Stanley.

"Life is not that simple, Sweetsong, You have already been admitted to a girls' school, when there was never a boy admitted here before you. You cannot have everything."

Stanley could hear Butter's purring from under the bed.

He raised his voice to drown out the sound. "I have always had everything," he said. "I even have a Rolls Royce back at Castle Sweet."

"But you are not there. You are here!" said Miss Rattray. "And you have made fun of the Betters by calling yourself the Butters. And now you are raising your voice to me, which is rude!"

"I'm sorry, ma'am."

WHACK! WHACK! WHACK!

"The Betters know better than to raise their voices at me, which is why they are better!"

"Why else are they better?" Stanley said over Butter's purring.

"They mind, for one thing!" Miss Rattray's own voice was raised now.

WHACK! WHACK! WHACK!

"They would never *dream* of sneaking down to the swimming pool, which is what I suspect *you* did, when you left *these* around the corner in the Changing Room!"

Miss Rattray tossed the clothing on Stanley's bed.

She stood and lumbered toward the door.

"*I* will stop that banging right now!" she said. "And *you* will call a halt to this Butter Club *right now*! I never want to hear of it again, Sweetsong! It is over!

And so are quick dips in the pool, when there is no one there to supervise you!"

WHACK! WHACK! WHACK!

Miss Rattray paused a moment in the doorway. "I will *not* send you home, either. I give up trying to get the cook to use the new computer, and I give up trying to get certain alumnae to contribute to the building fund, but I do *not* give up on my students! I will not give up on *you*, Sweetsong! That is not my way!"

Sixteen

Thursday night after the lights out bell, Josephine Jiminez was admitted to the school infirmary. She was suffering from a major stomachache, brought on by eating twelve Butterfingers.

"This is a disaster!" Stanley told Bagg, saying the word "disaster" in the same heavy tone his father had used the day moles invaded the great, green lawns of Castle Sweet. "The Butter Club is finished. Josephine Jiminez has come down with a bellyache. And the poor tarantula up in the Science Room will probably die from mishandling!"

"Wait a minute! Hold your horses!" said Stuart Bagg. "There is always a way out of any disaster."

"Lucy Lightite doesn't think so! Right after she saw you running naked from the Changing Room, she faxed her family to come and get her!"

"She will get over it," Bagg said. "And Josephine Jiminez will get over her bellyache, too. The only way to get on with it is to get over it!"

"The Butter Club is finished, though," Stanley moaned, sitting cross-legged on his bed in the dark, while Bagg looked through the closet for more clothes.

"The Butter Club is alive and well," said Bagg, slipping into a pair of Gap khakis. "The Butter Club must go underground, that's all."

"How can you dress in the dark?" said Stanley. "That's why you always forget your Hootie & The Blowfish T-shirt."

"That's my lucky shirt, but sometimes I like a change. And I never knew a boy with so many clothes."

"Are you poor, Bagg?"

"Where I come from clothes aren't too important. It's what's above, not what's below, it's what you know."

Bagg was always at his best in the dark. He found a neat green Lands' End shirt and pulled it over his head.

"Don't go swimming again, please," said Stanley.

"I won't," said Bagg, who had let him believe in Miss Rattray's theory that someone had gone into the pool. The next time he used the Changing Room, he would hide his human clothes up in the rafters.

"We can't go underground. Josephine ate all the Butterfingers there were. We can't wear one yellow sock or Miss Rattray will know. How will we have style? Or flair?" Stanley Sweetsong's face was not a happy one.

But Bagg was always an optimist.

Bagg knew from experience never to give up.

"You must have a secret location and do everything

in secret," he told Stanley. "You must have a secret handshake. And buy more Butterfingers!" Bagg's nose twitched at the thought of Butterfinger crumbs.

"I don't think Josephine is up to it," said Stanley. "And tomorrow her shrink comes. If we go underground, she may have to tell him about it."

"I don't think she will, Stanley."

"But shrinks can get secrets out of you," said Stanley. "My mother had a shrink once and when my father said don't tell him what we're worth or he'll charge more, my mother said he'd only get it out of her. They're very clever, Bagg. And we'll never know if Josephine tells him."

"I'll find out for you, Stanley."

"No one can find out what someone else tells a shrink," Stanley said.

"I can find out. What kind of a pal would I be if I couldn't?"

Now Bagg was dressed, and ready to sneak back to the Changing Room. It was risky enough scooting along the darkened corridors, but at least with clothes on he would not cause some frightened female to fax an SOS to her folks. He could pretend he was a friend who had visited Stanley and forgotten the time. Bagg would think of something if the occasion arose. The important thing was to get back to the Macintosh, before Drainboard began to fret. Then tomorrow, as Shoebag, he would sit in on Josephine's session with her shrink.

"Remember, Stanley: To get on with it, get over it. You have nothing to worry about anymore."

"But I can't always stop. Right now I'm worrying about the tarantula. I feel so sorry for her, Bagg."

Stuart Bagg felt a shiver down the length of his body.

He could not bring himself to discuss the tarantula. Of all arachnids, the tarantula was said to be the fiercest hunter. Its very hairs aided it in locating prey.

Bagg could barely bring himself to discuss an ordinary spider, but a fearsome one like the tarantula made his human stomach turn . . . for once a roach, *always* a roach (except for Gregor Samsa).

"Nevermind the tah-tah-tarantula," Bagg managed to spit out the word somehow.

"Have you seen her, Bagg?"

"No, fortunately."

"She's very beautiful," said Stanley Sweetsong. "I think you'd feel fortunate to see her . . . Bagg? Bagg? . . . Are you still here?"

He was not.

Seventeen

I t was Friday.
    Stretched out on a couch in the infirmary was Josephine Jiminez.

Behind her, in a large leather armchair, sat Dr. Dingle.

"Do you want to tell me about the Butter Club?" he said.

"I'm hungry. Do you have anything to eat?"

"Now, Josephine, you know we never eat in our sessions. And you just recovered from stomach trouble."

"That was last night. I'm back to normal."

"We'll see about that," said Dr. Dingle, who was not fond of the word "normal." In his profession it was not a money-producing word, and he rarely heard it when he didn't sneeze. Perhaps he was slightly allergic to it.

"Achoo!"

"God bless you," said Josephine.

"Why don't we end this session with a few words from you about the Butter Club," he persisted.

"Miss Rattray says there's no such club. . . . Anyway, why don't you get Stanley Sweetsong in here? He's been having nightmares about being put in one of Mr. Longo's tanks."

"*You* are my client, dear, not Stanley Sweetsong. Have *you* had any interesting dreams?"

His voice had such a plaintive sound, very like Josephine's father's every time he announced another transfer to a new Army post.

"I dreamed," Josephine began, "that on Career Day a famous actor came to talk to us in assembly, and guess what, Dr. Dingle?"

"What?" the psychologist leaned forward, pencil ready over the pad he held on his lap.

"He asked if he could see a performance of *If You're Not In, You're Out!*"

Of course she had made all that up. She never remembered her dreams. And an actor was *never* invited to speak on Career Day. Just writers were. Just scientists were. Just lawyers were. Just accountants, musicians, and computer analysts. Just females were, never males!

But Josephine felt sorry for Dr. Dingle in these sessions. She wanted to say something he could make notes about . . . and she *had* always wished she could meet a real live actor. How long could she continue writing and performing her plays without some notion of what one was like?

"In your dream, did this famous actor see a performance of your play?" Dr. Dingle asked. "In this dream how did you feel when the actor asked to see it?"

But Josephine was bored with the whole idea of this dream she never had. She uncrossed and crossed her legs, and put her palms behind her head and yawned.

"Well?" Dr. Dingle asked again.

"That's all there was to the dream."

"How do you feel about that dream?"

"I feel that we ought to have an actor come on Career Day, and I wish you'd tell Miss Rattray that."

Dr. Dingle made a note of it.

"What else, Josephine?" Dr. Dingle asked.

"Nothing. I feel quite normal today."

"Achoo!"

"God bless you."

Up the wall, beside the couch, a cockroach had paused, his antennae quivering, his eyes alert, almost as though he understood every word being spoken.

"We have a little visitor in here listening to everything we say," Josephine said.

The cockroach hurried away.

"You know, Josephine," said Dr. Dingle, "it is a good thing to have a lively imagination. Your little plays, your new little club, this little visitor you claim is present — all of that has its value. *But —*" he paused to rub his eyes, and take a deep breath.

"But?" Josephine said.

"But we must get to the bottom of things. Your rage, and your fears. The strange names you gave your dolls!"

One thing Josephine Jiminez was not afraid of was bugs. She looked out for them whenever she could. She watched the cockroach until it disappeared down the side of the couch.

"Tell me what you're thinking about right now." said Dr. Dingle, never one to give up on a client.

"I'm thinking of what it would be like to be a cockroach."

"Aha! Is that what you feel like? Something shunned. Something no one wants around?" Dr. Dingle was sitting forward now, his eyes bright.

Josephine said, "I never said I felt like one. I said I wondered what it would be like to *be* one."

"Wouldn't you always be hungry? Wouldn't you have rage? Wouldn't you want to smash your dolls against the wall? Wouldn't you fear that no one would want you in a club?"

Josephine glanced up at the large clock on the infirmary wall. Three minutes to go before the session was over. Ten minutes to go before the nine members of the secret, new, underground, Butter Club met in the Music Room.

Josephine Jiminez was its president.

She had never been a president before, and while she would have liked to discuss her presidential problems with a shrink, she could not trust him not to tell Miss Rattray that the Butters had gone underground.

He told Miss Rattray everything. Miss Rattray told Josephine's parents everything. Josephine's parents thanked Miss Rattray by giving gifts to the school, which they bought dirt cheap at the Army PX.

The latest one had been a computer for the cook.

On her way to her session with Dr. Dingle, Josephine had seen them crating it for return to her family, since Cook could not learn it, nor even bear to look at it.

"Continue, please, Josephine."

"I'm thinking, Doctor."

Josephine would have to cope with club problems herself.

On her own, she would have to deal with the fact that it would be very hard to be both the president of the Butters *and* the director, producer, and lead playwright of the Black Mask Theater.

A lot would be expected of her!

"If *I* were a cockroach," Dr. Dingle was pleased as punch with his new insight, "I would want to be *anything* but a cockroach!"

Josephine's hands went from behind her head down to the pockets of her blazer. Had she kept the receipt for the new box of Butterfingers? Stanley had said there would be dues, so that she would be paid back for all that she was spending on the candy. She would have to decide the amount and collect it from the members.

She had so much responsibility in her new situation.

"Well, what about it, Josephine?" the doctor said. "Isn't that how a cockroach thinks?"

"I suppose," Josephine answered, though she had lost the gist of the conversation by then.

"Finally!" said Dr. Dingle. "Now we're getting somewhere! Someday, if we continue to progress, you may forget all about your dolls. Or if you must have dolls, you might give them dolly names like Barbie, Suzy, or Betty Lou."

"My parents gave me those dolls," said Josephine. "Every time we got transferred to a new post, I got one. I got Monroe when we moved to Fort Monroe. I got one when we moved to Alexandria, Virginia. I got one when we moved to Fort Sam Houston, and when we moved to Washington, DC. And when we moved to Arlington, Virginia; Heidelberg, Germany; Huntsville, Alabama, and Seoul, Korea. That's how they got their names."

But Dr. Dingle was eyeing the clock, then shuffling papers as he always did at the end of a session.

"Time is up!" he called out "Never mind your dolls, Josephine. Next session we'll talk more about why you feel like a cockroach!"

Eighteen

There was nothing as exhausting as a session with a shrink!

Shoebag longed to head for Josephine Jiminez's room, where he could curl up for a brief nap in the ear of Monroe, the masked Kewpie doll.

But first, he must stop by the Macintosh, for a brief game of hide-and-seek with Radio and Garbage Pail.

As concerned as he was about his human friends, he was not one to forget his roach family.

His human clothes were hidden in the Changing Room. That night after dark, he would become Bagg again. He would meet with Stanley, and tell him Josephine had not told the shrink anything about the underground Butters.

Trudging past the Music Room, he saw the Butters heading in for their first meeting. And he saw Butter, the cat, sprawled on the piano top, licking his paws contentedly.

But as he went down the steps leading to the kitchen, his antennae lifted, and his cerci shuddered.

There was something in the air: something familiar and foul.

He could hear Cook telling someone, "Don't get that stuff in my kitchen! Hear me?"

A man's voice answered her, "Just tell me where the roaches were."

"I told you!" Cook was in her usual bad mood. "They were in the computer, but the computer is gone!"

Gone? With his entire family inside?

Shoebag's reflexes quickened with the panic he felt throbbing under his shell.

Not only was his family gone, but in an instant he knew the source of the foul odor.

It was Zap! Cooks's conversation was with the Zap man, the much feared world-class fumigator.

ZAP ZAPS COCKROACHES DEAD!

ZAP . . . FOR THINGS THAT DON'T DESERVE TO LIVE!

Shoebag would never forget those heartless slogans.

As fast as his six legs could carry him, he fled under the door of the Changing Room.

He must try to become Bagg again, only suddenly Shoebag felt himself falter. His tiny legs collapsed under him. He struggled for breath. With great effort he dragged himself back under the door to the hall.

"Just do that little room where the computer was!" Cook was shouting at the Zap man.

"I *did* the little room!"

"What you did was the Changing Room!" the cook answered.

Shoebag fastened himself against the light socket near the hall floor. He fell off it immediately, dizzy from the poisonous dose of Zap he had been exposed to in the Changing Room.

Shell-side down, legs up, he struggled for the strength to flip over, and flee.

"Close the kitchen door, Cook!" the Zap man called out. "I'm getting ready to zap the varmints!"

"I just step on them!" Shoebag heard Cook say, and he wiggled his antennae weakly, in protest.

Nineteen

It had been ten days since Stanley Sweetsong had seen Bagg. Sometimes he wondered if his pal had been only a mirage. Mr. Longo talked about optical illusions in science: sheets of water that seemed to appear in deserts. Tricks of the eye, aided by imagination.

Had Stuart Bagg been such a thing? Could a mirage leave behind a Hootie & The Blowfish T-shirt?

Now the October days in Pennsylvania had turned cold suddenly. But it was always nice and toasty in the Music Room. And thanks to Bagg the Music Room was not just warmth and rhythm. At certain times its operas and concertos masked the meetings of the underground Butters.

The girls and Stanley Sweetsong gave one another the secret handshake with thumbs-up and touching.

"Ahoy!" they chorused. "We're Butter!"

Josephine Jiminez called the meeting to order.

"Attention everyone!" said Josephine Jiminez. "We

will now have roll call. Ethel Lampert, a founding member, will take charge."

"Sweetsong!"

"Here!"

"Jiminez!"

"Here!"

"Greenwald!"

"Here!"

On and on down the list, all of their yellow Butter badges were pinned under the lapels of their blazers. The one yellow sock each member wore was also hidden, under a regulation white sock.

After roll call, Stanley Sweetsong stood and addressed the gathering.

"As you know we are secret secret!" He yawned and rubbed his eyes.

"We are *not* sleepy sleepy, however," said Josephine Jiminez. "Did you have another of your nightmares, Vice President Sweetsong?"

"Yes. I dreamed again that there was a fourth tank in Mr. Longo's Science Room, and *I* was in it."

"Pull yourself together, Vice President Sweetsong! We have club business to attend to!" Josephine Jiminez said.

Stanley Sweetsong straightened his shoulders and blinked his eyes, continuing. "The rumor is that C. Cynthia Ann Flower suspects that the Butters still exist!"

"Ha!" snorted Millie Greenwald. "She can't believe she's not Butter!"

"Butters are better than Betters!" the club members

chorused. "Betters cannot believe they're not Butters!"

"We have to be on guard," said Stanley Sweetsong.

"I would like to put that tarantula in C. Cynthia Ann's bed!" said Cleo Kanowitz.

"That poor tarantula is suffering enough in that stuffy tank!" Stanley said. "I would like to set him free. And the African frog, too, and the king snake! . . . No wonder I have bad dreams!"

Josephine Jiminez gave Stanley Sweetsong the elbow and said impatiently, "Make the major announcement."

"The major announcement," said Stanley Sweetsong, "is that Miss Rattray has asked an actor to come for Career Day."

"An *actor!?*" Cleo Kanowitz said. "We have never had an actor here!"

"Exactly!" said Josephine. "But now one is coming, thanks to my shrink! I believe he thinks it will control my rage."

"So you won't be the Doll Smasher anymore," said Stanley.

"Yes," Josephine agreed, "although with all my new duties, the Black Mask Theater has had very few performances lately."

Just like Stuart Bagg, the whacking of the walls was no more, too.

"The Butters," Josephine continued, "are underground. But there is no sense being underground if above ground no one knows you still exist. So we must plan something dramatic to do on Career Day!"

"An *actor!*" Cleo Kanowitz couldn't get over it. "A famous actor?"

"Fairly famous," said Josephine Jiminez.

"But not *that* famous," said Stanley.

"We must come out of hiding on Career Day with a bang!" said Josephine.

"What actor?" Cleo Kanowitz said.

"Everyone's favorite," said Josephine. "He is the spokesboy for Great Breath chewing gum."

"He's C. Cynthia Ann's favorite, not *mine*! You call *him* an actor?" Cleo Kanowitz was the argumentative type, a saucy little blonde from New York. "Gregor Samsa just does that one commercial! All he says over and over is 'Does your smile smell?'"

"*I* didn't choose him," said Josephine. "Miss Rattray did. Now let us put our heads together and decide on a plan of action."

Stanley Sweetsong closed his eyes as his father always did when *he* was concentrating on something very serious. (Should our next car be an Infiniti or a Porsche?)

Everyone was silent, except for Cleo Kanowitz, still saying "Gregor Samsa" to herself, making a face as though she had just smelled something putrid.

Stanley thought and thought, but it was hard to concentrate, hard not to think of Bagg.

Bagg would know what to do. He could come up with an answer as easily as he fit into Stanley's clothes. And Stanley missed that, too, having another boy around. Having a pal.

Twenty

S ometimes Cook had to tidy the halls herself, a task she felt was beneath her.

What she did was sweep them, then scoop it all up with her Dustbuster and put it back in its slot without emptying it.

It was pitch-dark inside.

There was not just dust in there, but also lint, the corpses of a cricket, and a fly, the leg of a spider and half his dragline, a paper clip, a third of a Life Saver, a yellow M & M, and Shoebag.

Awake, Shoebag said the Cockroach Prayer for the Dead, for he was sure that he would die.

"Go to a better life," he murmured, licking the M & M, shifting his shell away from the burden of the paper clip.

When Shoebag could sleep, he dreamed that Under The Toaster was scowling at him, saying "I TOLD YOU SO!" and pushing Drainboard aside as she held out her legs to embrace Shoebag. But there was only one real leg with him in the Dustbuster: the spider's hideous, hairy one.

Sick as Shoebag still was from the Zap dose, he was even sicker thinking of his family en route somewhere without him.

Sick as Shoebag was from this tragic blow by the Fickle Finger of Fate, he wondered if he would ever see Stanley Sweetsong again. Or ever again be Stuart Bagg.

Knowing Cook's lazy ways, knowing she hated emptying the Dustbuster, Shoebag forced down the fly corpse, thinking of it as his last meal. For the piece of Life Saver was too hard to chew, and the M & M was licked down to a sliver.

How could he eat a cricket which was from the noble old order of orthoptera, as Shoebag was himself?

Twenty-one

That Sunday, after church and before Sunday dinner, Stanley Sweetsong called home.

"What a strange name for a club," said his mother.

"And why are you only the VP?" his father said. "Why aren't you the P?"

"Because Josephine Jiminez is the P."

"She's only the P because her father is a famous general, I'll bet," said Mrs. Sweetsong.

"She's a good president," Stanley defended her. Not only good, but also in agreement with Stanley about what the Butters would do on Career Day.

"In an all-girl school," said Mr. Sweetsong, "what chance does one boy have when they vote for a president?"

"There was no vote," said Stanley.

"No vote?" his father said. "What kind of a school is that?"

"It's changed since my day," said Mrs. Sweetsong. "In my day there was always a vote. And in my day

85

the parents did not get letter after letter asking for money."

"The school wants to build a larger Science Room," said Stanley, "so Mr. Longo can imprison more poor creatures in tanks."

"Now, *don't* dwell on those tanks in the Science Room!" said Mrs. Sweetsong. "That's all you write about in your letters. Snakes and frogs and whatnot in those tanks."

"And a tarantula, too, like Tattle's, only this one is a Mexican blonde!"

His father said, "What do you call two spiders who just got married?" Mr. Sweetsong was always trying to cheer up his only son and sole heir.

"What *do* you call two spiders who just got married?"

"Newlywebs," his father laughed.

But Stanley did not need that much cheering up where Mr. Longo and his ugly tanks were concerned. On Career Day the Butters would strike! One tank would be empty. They could not let the snake or the frog go free, for they had been captives too long. They would not know how to fend for themselves, and it would be impossible for the Butters to care for them.

But Stanley could care for the tarantula until Thanksgiving. Then he would take him home to Tattle, who knew all about this king of spiders!

And the Mexican blonde was the perfect choice, since it had been donated to the Science Room by none other than C. Cynthia Ann Flower.

There *had* been a vote on that, and it was unanimous!

In honor of Gregor Samsa, there would be nine glowing smiles on the faces of the Butters, and none of the smiles would smell.

The tarantula would have a new, safe home, and to replace him in the tank, there would be a Butterfinger.

"You haven't said you miss us," said Stanley's mother.

"You haven't said you wish you were back at Castle Sweet," said his father.

"I have been very busy," Stanley said.

"But never forget," his father said, "someday this will all be yours!"

"I can make my own bed now," Stanley said.

"You won't have to here," said Mrs. Sweetsong.

"But I am not there," said Stanley. "And I have eight friends here."

"Thanksgiving is coming," said Mrs. Sweetsong. "Then you will be here and not there."

"We'll have a big turkey!" his father said. "Where do all good turkeys go when they die?"

"Where?" Stanley asked.

"To oven!" his father laughed.

"Not funny," Stanley said, because one thing the Butters stood for was kindness to all critters large and small.

There was yet another reason for the Butters to dislike C. Cynthia Ann Flower. For there she was, on that blustery Autumn noon, as Stanley came out of the phone booth, dressed in her royal blue blazer, white skirt, and white sock and red sock. A fur collar on her parka. Rabbit fur, it looked like to Stanley Sweetsong.

So he said to her, "Anyone who's better, ought to

have a better idea to keep warm than wearing the fur of a dead animal."

"Anyone who was butter," she replied, "was melted down by Miss Rattray into a yellow puddle, and no longer exists. Isn't that right, Stanley?"

She opened her parka and flashed her white button with the red letters: WE'RE BETTER!

Next to it was a button with Gregor Samsa's photo on it, for C. Cynthia Ann Flower was a big fan of the Great Breath spokesboy.

Her beautiful beautiful face smiled meanly at Stanley.

She said, "For a while I thought the Butter Club was meeting secretly, but the meltdown finished you, didn't it?"

Stanley wished he could laugh in her beautiful beautiful face, but the Butters were an underground club, and underground people kept their cool, and waited for just the right moment to strike.

Career Day.

C. Cynthia Ann Flower would be in for a little Butter Surprise the second week in November.

Now everything was working out.

The only thing missing was Bagg.

Twenty-two

At the end of October, the Betters treated the Lower School to pizza at Pie in the Sky, for Patsy Southgate's birthday.

Everyone went but Stanley Sweetsong.

He did not like to be the only boy along on these treks to town.

He stayed in his room, playing a game on his computer, guiding a speeding car through a treacherous course. Eating a Butterfinger, the official candy of the Butters. Talking to Butter, who had taken to hanging out in the dustballs under Stanley's bed.

He was surprised that Josephine joined the group.

He was amazed that the Black Mask Theater had not had a single performance in a month!

Josephine did not even like Patsy Southgate, nor any other Better. But all the Butters were going, and Josephine said since the VP wouldn't go, the P would have to.

"I thought I'd find you here," said Miss Rattray, standing in the doorway. "May I come in?"

"Yes, ma'am . . . I did not feel like having pizza."

"Sometimes it's hard to be the only boy, isn't it?" She sat down on Stanley's bed.

"Not all the time it isn't," he said.

He turned around in his desk chair and faced her.

The tip of Butter's tail protruded under the dust cover, whipping the floor impatiently.

Miss Rattray never saw things she had to look down to see. She had no inkling the cat was studying her ankles with an eye to batting one with his paw.

Stanley was devoted to Butter now. The cat seemed to favor him, and preferred to spend most of his time in Stanley's room.

"You have learned to make your bed in a proper way, Stanley," said Miss Rattray, "Congratulations!"

"Thank you. I only make my own bed here, though. At Castle Sweet a maid does that."

"Do you miss Castle Sweet?"

"I used to."

"And now?"

"Not so much," said Stanley.

What was she doing there, he wondered? Had she heard about the underground Butters?

Had she waited until everyone in the Lower School was gone to tell him she'd found out what was going on in the Music Room certain afternoons?

"One can learn to do without servants," said Miss Rattray. "I sometimes think we are too dependent on them here . . . and they are not always dependable. Even this very morning I had to speak to Cook about emptying the Dustbuster. Cook believes she shouldn't be expected to do anything but cook!"

"Yes, ma'am."

"But we all have little extra duties, some we don't foresee. And that is why I'm here, Stanley. I have a surprise for you."

"Is it a good surprise or a bad one?"

"A good one, I think. I want you to be Gregor Samsa's student escort on Career Day. You will help me greet him, and then you will be his guide while he's with us."

"Fine," said Stanley. "That *is* a good surprise."

"Have you ever met an actor before?"

"No, ma'am, but I have chewed Great Breath gum."

"Not here, though," said Miss Rattray, her eyes narrowing.

"No. At Castle Sweet I chewed it."

"Because *we* don't chew gum, do we?"

"No, ma'am, we don't."

Miss Rattray rose, "Gregor Samsa is not much of an actor, but he has had other small parts in theater, though not big parts."

"Then why was he picked for Career Day?"

"He is popular with the girls, and Great Breath chewing gum is making a donation to our building fund."

"So there can be more tanks in the Science Room," Stanley said gloomily.

"More educational exhibits, yes," Miss Rattray agreed. "All right, then, Stanley, I am counting on you. Go back to your game. The girls should return soon from Pie in the Sky."

Stanley could hear the girls. He could hear the laughter of Josephine Jiminez. This was a rare sound, unless she was playing the part of Monroe, the masked Kewpie doll who always told the others they were not good enough to get in the club. But in Monroe's voice, the laughter was mean, not high and happy as it sounded now from next door.

Then, suddenly, Stanley heard Josephine wail, even louder than the wail she had let out at the news C. Cynthia Ann Flower was president of both school clubs!

"Oh, no!" she called out.

And Butter, who could not tolerate sudden noises, shot out from under the bed, running hair-raised to the door.

"No! No! No!" Josephine Jiminez yelled.

But she did not whack the wall.

She was not putting on a play at all.

Whatever had happened, had to be real.

Twenty-three

"Why were you wailing, Josephine?" Stanley asked.

"I just read a letter from my mother. Listen to this!"

Dearest Daughter,

We are coming for Career Day. Are you surprised? Your father and I have another surprise for you, too. We have been thinking long and hard about how unhappy you are at school. We never realized what all our moving about the world has done to you. Then last week we had a conversation with Dr. Dingle that helped us make a decision.

Darling, why didn't you ever tell us that you felt like a cockroach — something no one wants around? No wonder you are often lonely and angry!

Your father has decided to take early retirement from the Army. We are making plans to buy a house in Knoxville (known for coal, marble, aluminum sheeting, and textiles), Tennessee, where your father grew up. On Career Day we will take you home with us. It will be the last day you have to spend at Miss Rattray's.

So cheer up, dear daughter, you will never again feel like a cockroach. You will be our little girl. . . . The decision is final.

Love, Mother.

P.S. You'd better start packing! See you in three weeks!

"I never knew you felt like a cockroach," Stanley said as Josephine slapped the letter down on her desk.

"I never felt like one is why you never knew it!" said Josephine. "What is to become of me?"

Stanley moved Arlington, Monroe, and Washington out of the way and sat down on the bed. "And what is to become of the Black Mask Theater?" he asked.

"I don't care about that so much. We haven't had a performance in weeks."

"I know. You haven't whacked the walls in a long time."

"A president has more things to do than put on the same play over and over," said Josephine.

"You'd better fax your mother and tell her you do not want to move to Tennessee."

"Tennessee is one of the few states where we have never lived! I know nothing about Tennessee!"

"The Sweetsongs have visited every state in the U.S.

of A.," said Stanley Sweetsong, remembering a riddle his father had told him when they were tooling through Nashville, Tennessee, in their Rolls Royce. "What did Tennessee, Josephine?"

"What *did* Tennessee?"

"She saw what Arkansas."

"Not funny!" Josephine said. "And it will do no good to fax my mother. In our family, when a decision is final, it is final!"

"Fax her anyway," said Stanley. "Tell her you like it here."

"I never said I like it here!"

"But you *do*, don't you, Josephine?"

Josephine Jiminez sat down on the bed beside Alexandria, the wooden doll with pink-rouged cheeks. She frowned as she thought over Stanley's question.

"I never did before," she said. "I was never part of the 'in' crowd." Then she grabbed the masked Kewpie doll, Monroe, and said in his deep, stern voice, "If you're not in, you're out," but there was none of the old anger, only sadness in her tone. And she did not smash any doll against the wall.

Twenty-four

Every other month, the Betters sang in assembly.
This sunny November morning, after the school
song, and before Miss Rattray's announcements, C.
Cynthia Ann Flower led them out on the stage.

"One, two, three!" she said, and then she waved
her arms to get the performance underway.

> *We are the Betters*
> *Better at Everything!*
> *Better when we dance and when we sing!*
> *Better at everything!*
> *Better at science and history,*
> *Better at solving a mystery,*
> *Better than a queen, better than a king,*
> *Better at everything!*
> *We're Betters!*
> *We look better, read a book better,*
> *Swim a brook better, and we cook better,*
> *We are the Betters!*

C. Cynthia Ann Flower then found a seat in the audience, right next to Josephine Jiminez.

"If the Butters had been better, you might have been up on stage yourself, Josephine. But not everyone can be better, particulary a Doll Smasher like you."

Josephine said nothing, for she was in a slump.

She was imagining herself somewhere in Tennessee going to another new school, seeing more unfamiliar faces, hearing some new teacher say, "We have a new girl in our midst, so everyone welcome her," which no one would do.

On the other side of Josephine sat Stanley Sweetsong. He leaned over Josephine and said to C. Cynthia Ann Flower, "Just you wait!"

"Wait for what? Wait for you to get taller so you'll be the size of other ten-year-olds? For Josephine to lose some of her freckles so we can see her face? Haw! Wait for *what*?"

Now Miss Rattray was standing before the assembly waiting for absolute silence.

"I have two announcements!" she said. "One is that we are losing Josephine Jimenez after Career Day, and we are sorry to lose her."

"We *are*?" C. Cynthia Ann Flower muttered under her breath. "I don't know anyone who is."

"The other announcement," said Miss Rattray, "is that Stanley Sweetsong will be the personal escort of Gregor Samsa when he comes for Career Day next week. Anyone who wants to shake the hand of this famous spokesboy and actor must go through Stanley."

C. Cynthia Ann Flower's hand went up instantly.

"Yes, dear?"

"But a Better has *always* been the personal escort!"

"This year, since we are asking a *male* actor, we shall have a *male* escort, dear! There is no male Better."

"There is no male better than me!" Stanley Sweetsong whispered at C. Cynthia Ann Flower.

Now there were two of Miss Rattray's girls in a slump that morning. One with the dread of starting all over again in Tennessee. The other with the dream of meeting Gregor Samsa dimming.

Twenty-five

H ow would *they* like it," Under The Toaster used to say of humans, "if someday creatures a hundred times their size gassed them — *pffft* — like they were mindless, heartless, unfeeling flecks of flesh, put on earth only to annoy them?"

Shoebag's heart broke remembering his father's tirades against the human race.

Ever since he had come flying out of the Dustbuster, into the kitchen wastebasket, he had wondered what would become of him, alone in this place, without a family or another roach anywhere in view.

How could he think of being Bagg again? Why would he want to become the very enemy who had uprooted his family's home, invented a noxious substance like Zap (which had nearly killed him), and through the years stepped on his kind, designed lethal Roach Motels for his kind, and always looked upon any critter from roachdom with loathing?

Still, one thing cockroaches were known for was

loyalty. Gas them, they would return. Smoke them out, they would be back. Tear down their buildings, they would remain in the neighborhood.

And so it was that Shoebag, frail and shaken from everything that had happened to him, found himself finally back in the Changing Room.

"You have to judge humans individually," Drainboard was fond of saying. "One in a million is decent."

Shoebag believed Stanley was one of those one in a million.

High in the eaves of the small room were the clothes Bagg had hidden so many weeks ago . . . before he had been orphaned and Zapped.

Now came the next step: "Flit, flutter, quiver, quaver, totter," and as always, on the word "totter" he felt himself begin the change.

Twenty-six

Sometimes, if you put the top of a water glass to a wall, and place your ear against its bottom, you can hear everything that is being said in the room next door to you.

That night after dinner, Josephine Jiminez could.

She heard everything C. Cynthia Ann Flower had to say to Stanley Sweetsong.

Butter sat on her bed watching this strange behavior, his yellow eyes alert and curious.

"I just dropped by to see how you are, Stanley."

"I am okay, C. Cynthia Ann. Why do you ask?"

"I ask because I've been thinking about you. . . . You know, Stanley, the Betters have never had a boy member."

"There has never been a boy, until me, at Miss Rattray's School for Girls," he said.

"If a boy was a Better, things would be better for him than they ever have been before."

"How would they be better?"

"You would sit in the front row at all school performances. That's better, isn't it?"

"Yes, that's better."

"You would help Miss Rattray decide what new students to enroll next year . . . possibly another boy. That's better, isn't it?"

"Possibly another boy?" said Stanley Sweetsong. "That really *is* better!"

"Even if the Butters were *not* melted down, they could never get another boy enrolled here. They had no power," said C. Cynthia Ann Flower. "We have all the power!"

"This is true," Stanley Sweetsong agreed.

Josephine Jiminez's eyes filled with tears.

"And something else might happen, too," said C. Cynthia Ann Flower. "I *am* the president of the Science Club, so possibly you could send for something from Bugs Alive, and I could vote for it to win a prize."

"Then I would belong to both clubs," said Stanley Sweetsong. "And then I would have a key to the Science Room!"

"Then you would. Then you would not miss that freckle-faced frump from next door at all!"

Josephine Jiminez felt her ears burn.

"And she will be gone, anyway, Stanley," said C. Cynthia Ann.

"This is true. She will be in Tennessee."

"Good riddance to bad rubbish!" said C. Cynthia Ann Flower. "And all I ask in return is to meet Gregor Samsa."

Josephine Jiminez could not stand to hear another word. She set the water glass down hard on her desk, causing Butter to flinch and whip his tail.

Monroe was still not packed, though all the other dolls were. Monroe was her favorite of all the Cast of Characters. He was the only one she never smashed against the wall. She sat down on her bed and put the small Kewpie doll on her lap.

"You are the only friend I have," she told it. "Right this very moment the friend I thought I had is making friends with my worst enemy. He didn't even wait for me to be gone, Monroe."

Monroe's gruff voice answered, "Well, if you're not in, you're out. . . . Who knows that better than the two of us?"

Then suddenly, Butter saw a shadow under the floor, something just outside.

He leapt from the bed, crouched low, ears cocked forward.

"What is it, Butter?"

The cat let out a high little mew, eyes narrowed to green slits.

"Is someone there?"

Josephine Jiminez flung open the door.

"*Who* are *you*?"

"Stuart Bagg."

The two of them stared at each other, for who with red hair and freckles would not stare back at someone else with red hair and freckles?

Twenty-seven

Josephine liked Stuart Bagg a lot. She liked him because he looked like her. She liked him because
Butter seemed to like him, too, following after him,
rubbing against him. She liked him because he did not
kill the jumping spider who had let down his dragline
over her bureau.

The only thing she didn't like about him was the
faint odor of his clothes.

"Raid?" she asked.

"Zap," he said. "They fumigated the area down-
stairs by the kitchen where I came in."

"Yes, because Cook saw some roaches near the
Macintosh they're returning to my family," said
Josephine.

He was such a polite boy and, for a boy, unusually
curious about her family — where they lived and why
the computer was being sent to them.

She sat on the bed beside him, telling him all about
it . . . and more, as well. She told him about life as an

Army brat, and about all the moves her family had made, all the schools she had been in and out of, and how now there was yet another move, just as she was making friends.

"Just as I became a president," she said. "Are you a new boy? I thought there was only Stanley Sweetsong enrolled here."

"I am a new boy, but not here," he told her. "I am Stanley's pal."

"And that is another thing," — Josephine was in a mood to confide — "Stanley Sweetsong has already switched his loyalty to my great enemy C. Cynthia Ann Flower, and I am not even gone yet. So you can't count on him to stay your pal."

"Yes, you can. He would not be taken in by her." Now Butter was sitting on the down comforter licking his lips and staring at Bagg, as though Bagg was not a boy but a can of Fancy Feast.

"Things change in this life, Stuart Bagg. Things do and people do."

"That's the only way to get over it and get on with it," said Stuart Bagg.

"I'll never get over Stanley Sweetsong making friends with my enemy," she said. "And I'll never get over not being a P again."

"You might become a Q. A Q is better than a P. And a Q comes after a P."

"A Q?"

"A queen. You might be queen of something."

"In Tennessee? There are no queens in Tennessee."

"I know a little about change myself," said Stuart Bagg, "and here is what I know. I know you think you won't like what's ahead, but what's ahead can be magical."

"In *Tennessee*?"

"Even there. Magic can happen anywhere."

"The only magic in my life is what I make myself, and I don't have the heart for it, anymore."

"Magic can, magic is, magic will, will, will . . ."

"Will what?"

"Will, will, oh, oh. Oh, oh."

Butter sprang from the bed, for his eye had suddenly caught a wee cockroach scrambling along the floor.

The jumping spider saw it, too. It stopped in its tracks, its two front legs raised expectantly.

Where Stuart Bagg had sat, there was only a slight indentation left on the bedspread, one that soon disappeared just as he had — *pffft*.

On the bed, with Josephine, there was only Monroe.

On the floor there was a pair of Gap khakis, a green Lands' End shirt, white boxer shorts, and Doc Martens.

Twenty-eight

Career Day was so close to Thanksgiving, few parents attended.

Retired General Pedro Jiminez and his wife came, of course, for they were there to fetch Josephine.

The Flowers were present, of course, for the Flowers were so proud of their daughter, C. Cynthia Ann, that they never missed a school function.

Ethel Lampert's mother came, for she was curious about the great change that had come over her daughter so suddenly. A child who had once lived for stamps was now little interested even in the rare purple-and-white Klotzhorn stamp from Austria. What was *that* all about?

As the parents gathered for tea in Miss Rattray's salon on the main floor of the Upper School, Stanley Sweetsong walked toward the Music Room with Josephine. There was to be a last-minute meeting of the underground Butters.

"Whatever's become of Stuart Bagg?" said Stanley. "He was right when he told you I would never fall for C. Cynthia Ann's malarkey."

"That wasn't how he put it. He was too mysterious to say 'malarkey.'"

"He's probably so mysterious he's not even real."

"He has to be if we both saw him."

"I never saw him just *pfffft* disappear before my eyes like you did. But those *are* my clothes he left behind. And I still have his Hootie & The Blowfish shirt."

Josephine said firmly, "He's real."

"Then why hasn't he been back to see us?"

"Because nothing real lasts," said Josephine.

"What about me being in this school? Won't I last?"

"That's *un*real. One boy in an all-girls' school."

"What about our plan to give the tarantula a better life?"

"Are you sure *you* want to do it? Are you sure you don't want to be a Better, and a member of the Science Club?"

"The only reason I was nice to C. Cynthia Ann was so it will be easier for me to get the key from her."

"Aha! The key to the Science Room! That was what you were after!"

"I have everything ready for the Mexican blonde. I've covered the tank with Bagg's lucky T-shirt, too."

"I hope he doesn't need it."

"He said clothes weren't important where he lives."

"But *lucky* clothes might be," said Josephine.

"Maybe that's why he left it behind. So *I'll* get lucky."

Into the Music Room the pair went to make plans for the Butters' first public act.

The moment they were inside, all the other Butters stood and clapped for Josephine.

It was their way of showing respect for the P who would soon be leaving them.

Josephine had never received a standing ovation before and she was so overwhelmed Stanley had to begin the meeting.

"Here is the plan," he said. "I will tell C. Cynthia Ann Flower she can take my place as Gregor Samsa's escort after he speaks in assembly. Since everyone will then go to the Science Room to see the prizewinners, I will take the key, unlock the door, and welcome everyone."

"I get it!" Josephine spoke up. "She will think you have made that arrangement so she can be alone with her idol!"

"Exactly!" said Stanley. "And while Gregor gives his speech, I will have to get the Mexican blonde up to my room safely."

Cleo Kanowitz spoke up. "But she will know you swiped the tarantula from the tank!"

"She may know it," Stanley said, "but, remember, members of the Science Club are not supposed to lend their keys to anyone! She will not want to admit she lent it to me!"

"Very clever!" said Ethel Lampert. "'Will you leave a Butterfinger in the Mexican blonde's tank?"

"I will. And let everyone try to figure out what *that* means!" Stanley said.

"What if no one does?" Cleo asked.

"It is our first aboveground action," said Stanley. "There will be others, always with the Butterfinger on the scene. It will be the Butter Surprise. Eventually, someone will get it!"

"Rumors will spread," said Ethel Lampert.

"Whispers will be whispered," said Josephine, "and talk will start. Too bad I'll be in Tennessee and miss out on all of it!" She had meant it as a breezy, little nothing remark, but her voice had broken when she got to "Tennessee" and now she was thinking of war and famine and lost dogs to keep from crying over her own sad situation.

"TOO BAD!" everyone chorused.

"But I will write you all about it," Stanley promised.

"We all will!" they said. "We will never forget our P."

Ethel Lampert said, "We will not even appoint a new P. The Butters will be run by the VP."

"I will run the Butters," Stanley vowed, "but you will still be our P, Josephine."

The great outpouring of affection was too much for Josephine Jiminez. As a rush of stinging tears blinded her, she ran from the Music Room into the hall, where she collided with Dr. Dingle and his wife.

"I have never seen you cry before!" he told Josephine, his eyes wide with wonder.

His wife reminded him, "She *is* leaving today, dear. It's only normal —"

"Achoo!" Dingle sneezed. "Achoo!"

Twenty-nine

As happy as Shoebag was to witness the Butters' tribute to Josephine Jiminez, he could not feel cheerful about his own wretched condition.

With his entire family now moved in the Macintosh to Tennessee, he was orphaned.

Not only was he an orphan, something was interfering with the formula that took him back and forth from roachdom to the world of humans.

How had it happened that so suddenly, in the midst of his conversation with Josephine Jiminez, he had been *pffft*-changed back to his familiar self?

The only explanation Shoebag could come up with was that the dose of Zap had upset his system.

The Zap had also upset the natural order of bug life in the school. It always sent roaches scurrying to nearby buildings, other Orthopetera running for cover, and arachnids fleeing to safer ground.

That was how the jumping spider had found its way to Josephine Jiminez's room.

If there was anything more loathsome than a jumping spider, Shoebag had never met up with it. Back in Brooklyn, a jumping spider (with one leg missing, thanks to a Persian cat) had killed Coffee Cup, Shoebag's little brother. He had also used his dragline to tie up Drainboard. Only a miracle had saved her from becoming the jumping spider's breakfast.

Now another one of those nasty things was in hot pursuit of Shoebag. It had all eight of its legs, many eyes, and the old familiar spider's warcry: DEATH TO ALL INSECTS! Since spiders were arachnids and not insects, they enjoyed pointing this out when they charged their enemies.

Shoebag sulked and skulked around the halls and walls of the Lower School, often with Butter prowling around after both creatures.

For courage, Shoebag sang to himself a favorite old cockroach song.

We lurk around and on our mark, we come out in the dark.
Hey de hi ho, we don't need a coach
To get there!
He de hi ho, if you are a roach,
You'll get there!

We creep around and find the crumbs, happy to be chums,
Hey de hi ho, we hunt high and low,
In kitchens.
Hey de hi ho, the parties we throw,
In kitchens!

But it did not sound like a happy song, anymore.

Still, Shoebag never, ever, lost his hope altogether, for that was not his way.

And even in the darkest hour, a cockroach prayer was often heard by the Great Cockroach in the Sky.

How else to explain the astonishing news that Gregor Samsa himself was on his way to this place?

Gregor had rescued him before, and Shoebag believed that he would rescue him again, if there was only some way for him to get the spokesboy's attention.

For once a roach, always a roach, never mind that Gregor had abandoned roachdom for stardom!

If there were anyone who could help Shoebag, Gregor was that person!

Such were Shoebag's thoughts when the thin lariat of spider silk was thrown around his shell.

And pulled tight.

"DEATH TO ALL INSECTS!" Shoebag heard, as he fainted.

Thirty

Gregor Samsa was much taller than Stanley, and he was huskier, too.

He was also mysterious, for he wore very dark glasses, the kind with mirror lenses in which you saw your own reflection. And he had a strange, long nose, with a twitch to it, as though he was catching the scent of something wild. His hair was so short it was almost like a beard on his head, a bristle, and it was black as midnight.

But the spookiest thing about him was his voice, which was not as loud as it was deep, like a grown man's.

"Does your smile smell?" he asked Stanley, with a chuckle, and he handed him a package of gum. "Chew Great Breath!"

Stanley did not tell him that at Miss Rattray's School for Girls (and now one boy) no one chewed gum.

He pocketed the package and proceeded to show him around the school.

"And this is my room," Stanley said near the end of the tour.

"It's not a very big room, is it?" Gregor Samsa said.

There on Stanley's desk was the plastic container he had ready for the Mexican blonde. Over it was Bagg's Hootie & The Blowfish T-shirt.

"No, it's not a big room," said Stanley, pushing the container to one side, quickly.

"And you have no television," said Gregor Samsa, who was carrying a Watchman, which he turned on at every opportunity.

"But I have a computer," Stanley said, "and I have fifty games. . . . And back at my home, I have a hundred more."

"You should watch more television," said Gregor Samsa. "I watch it all the time, since I am a television actor."

"Where do you come from?" Stanley asked.

"I come from here and there. I used to go back and forth."

"I come from Castle Sweet," said Stanley. "I go back and forth. I will go forth for Thanksgiving, and then back here after."

Last Sunday Stanley had called Tattle's cottage at Castle Sweet, telling him he was bringing the Mexican blonde with him.

"Be very careful handling her, Stanley," Tattle had told him. "Nudge her gently into the palm of your hand. Don't let her fall, for her abdomen could burst!

Remember how I carried Weezer, and don't *over*handle her!"

Stanley had some potting soil ready in his closet, to put into the plastic container . . . and also a small rock for the Mexican blonde to hide behind.

He had put a square of screen where the neck of the T-shirt opened, so he could look in at her once he smuggled her from the Science Room.

So far, the only food Stanley had to offer the Mexican blonde was a dead roach, wrapped up in a spider's dragline. Stanley supposed it was the same poor roach he had seen in his room one evening when he was saying his prayers.

Stanley had found Butter batting it about under his desk, and even though tarantulas liked only live prey, Stanley knew he could get her to eat it if he jiggled it to make it look alive. So Stanley had dropped the roach into the container, near the rock.

Gregor had been staring at the mirror above Stanley's desk, his long fingers touching his mouth as though he was examining something there.

"Is anything wrong?" Stanley asked him.

"It's just the mirror," he answered. "I have never liked mirrors much."

Then he pulled himself together and said, "Carry on, Sweetsong!"

As Stanley and Gregor left the room and passed Josephine Jiminez's room, Butter darted out into the hall. He had probably been sniffing around, trying to find the captive roach.

"A cat!" Gregor Samsa jumped back.

"It's only Butter," said Stanley. "Butter won't hurt you."

"I've never trusted a cat," Gregor Samsa said.

"Butter wouldn't hurt a fly," Stanley told him.

"How about a roach?" Gregor Samsa asked with a slanted smile, as they kept walking along. "But I suppose there are no roaches in this school, hmmm?"

Stanley decided not to say there were. It would not be polite to tell a visitor roaches were around.

"No roaches," Stanley fibbed, as Butter scampered ahead of them.

"There probably are a few, though," Gregor Samsa said. "Roaches have been on this earth for two hundred-fifty million years. They were here two hundred-forty-nine million years before people were. They are great survivors."

At the bottom of the stairs, Miss Rattray's girls were squealing with joy at the sight of the spokesboy celebrity.

"I hope you don't mind giving autographs, Mr. Samsa," said Stanley.

"Gregor. Call me Gregor . . . and I don't mind. I like to be noticed! I like being a star!"

In every way but one, Gregor Samsa behaved like a star, too. But whoever heard of a star who did not like mirrors?

Thirty-one

I will be back to get you, Shoebag.

Of course, Stanley Sweetsong did not hear Gregor promise that. Stanley Sweetsong did not even know that Gregor had looked down the neck of the T-shirt and spotted Shoebag tied up in the bottom of the plastic container.

But roaches have not been around for 250 million years without picking up a few smart tricks.

Shoebag did not even have to open his mouthpiece to communicate with Gregor. Gregor did not have to open his mouth, either. Bug language is always silent.

Hold your horses, Gregor! I'm alive down here!

Shoebag? How did you wind up in a spider's dragline, old friend?

Never mind that. The formula isn't working, Gregor.

Did you say it on a Wednesday night?

Oh, oh, Shoebag had not always waited for dark, and not always for a Wednesday.

I was careless, Gregor.

You fouled up, did you? You may have lost your power to go back and forth forever.

I think I am going to be fed to a tarantula.

I will be back to get you, Shoebag.

So it was not Zap that had done him in.

It was his own foolhardy recklessness.

That fact would not have surprised Under The Toaster.

The very thought of his stern papa brought a shudder of longing to Shoebag's shell. He yearned to be free again, and to find his way to his family, somehow. Even if it meant going to Tennessee.

At least the lucky Hootie & The Blowfish T-shirt was over him. Now all he had to do was wait for Gregor.

But waiting for a star is always risky.

Thirty-two

"Here is the key to the Science Room," said C. Cynthia Ann Flower. "Don't lose it, Stanley, for I would be in deep *trouble* if anyone found out I gave it to you!"

Stanley knew she was nervous, for her hand was moist, as was the key she slipped to him. And she was excited, too, for now she was face-to-face with her idol, Gregor Samsa.

They stood backstage in the auditorium. Stanley introduced them.

"Pleased to meet you, C. Cynthia Ann Flower," said Gregor Samsa, whipping off his dark glasses, his long nose twitching with pleasure. "And my, my, my, you *are* a flower!"

"Tee-hee! Tee-hee!" giggled the president of the Science Club, and also the president of the Betters. "I have always wanted to meet you, Gregor."

Stanley said, "As soon as you are finished, Gregor,

C. Cynthia Ann will take you to the Science Room, where all the parents will be, and I will be."

Gregor Samsa shook his head. "As soon as I am finished speaking, I have a private errand I must take care of before I do anything else."

"A private errand?"said Stanley anxiously. "Can't it wait?" For timing was everything in this first Butter Surprise.

"It can't wait," Gregor Samsa said firmly.

"Oh, please, can't it wait?" C. Cynthia Ann begged him. Gregor Samsa frowned.

"Please?" C. Cynthia Ann begged him, knowing she might miss the chance to escort him down to see the prizewinners.

And what would Stanley do, if there was not time to get the delicate Mexican blonde up to his room?

"Please?" again from C. Cynthia Ann.

It was plain that Gregor Samsa could not resist her. The sharp edges of his long face softened. His nostrils quivered. His very deep voice rose slightly. "Oh, all right," he said. "But I cannot stay there long. I have this private errand."

It was time for Gregor to go out on the stage, while C. Cynthia Ann waited backstage.

It was time for Stanley to hurry across to Mr. Longo's room, unlock the door, and fetch the Mexican blonde. In her place, he would put the Butterfinger, which was already softened slightly from being in his back pocket.

As he ran from the auditorium, Stanley could hear the applause for Gregor Samsa.

121

Tarantulas are very quick, as well as very delicate.

Stanley remembered exactly how Tattle had handled Weezer.

Before he picked her up, he took some withered moths from the tank and wrapped them in a Kleenex.

"And I have some lettuce for you which I saved from lunch," he told the Mexican blonde. "And there is a roach, too." He did not say that it was dead.

Then he reached into the tank and took her up quickly, making sure that all of her eight legs left the ground at the same time.

Since being lifted up in such a manner was totally new to the Mexican blonde, she made herself become paralyzed.

"It's all right," Stanley told her. "I am rescuing you."

He slipped her into a small paper cup.

Then he dropped the Butterfinger down into the tank.

"It's all right," he kept whispering into the cup. "I have a safe place waiting for you."

Stanley could not bear to look at the king snake or the African frog.

Perhaps another time the Butters would release them, too, when they could find someone to take them in.

But right now, Stanley had to get the Mexican blonde up to his room, then hurry back to the Science Room.

When C. Cynthia Ann and Gregor arrived, along with the parents, Stanley had to be there, too. Be there, and act just as surprised as they would. Be there and exclaim, "A Butterfinger! But *where* is the tarantula?"

Thirty-three

PLOP!

"Gregor? Is that you?"

"My name is not Gregor. My name is Blonde."

Shoebag was bound and gagged shell-up, and could not immediately see who was there. "My name is —"

Blonde finished the sentence for him. "Dinner," she said. "Your name is 'Dinner,' and you look like a very tasty meal to me."

"Oh, no!" Shoebag moaned. "Not the tarantula?"

"*Cómo se va?*" said the Mexican blonde. "A *cucaracha*, hmmm? In that dreary tank there was nothing to eat but dead moths. You may have one for your last meal, if you wish. I believe the boy who rescued me dropped some in here with me."

"Thanks anyway," said Shoebag, "but I've lost my appetite."

"That can happen, *Cucaracha*. I'll have the lettuce

myself, then. I'll wrap it around your legs, if I can wait until dinner. Your legs are very tempting."

"Speaking of moths," said Shoebag, stalling for time "why did the moth eat through the carpeting?"

"You tell me," said Blonde.

"He wanted to see the floor show."

This made the creature laugh very, very hard.

She laughed so hard she spread out her long legs, and good grief, Shoebag saw one!

It was huge.

It was hairy.

It had black bottom leg segments.

It was a tarantula, all right!

Under The Toaster had seen one in *National Geographic* once, and come panting back from the library to say, "They even have fangs!"

Shoebag could not see her fangs. But his shell shook against the silk spider thread, and his antennae did a sorrowful dive.

"That was a good joke!" said the tarantula. "No one in the Science Room told jokes. There was nothing amusing in there, which was a pity, because we Mexican blondes like to have fun. Blondes always have more fun, you know. We're not serious like scientists."

Where was Gregor?

Thinking with the speed roach minds are known for, Shoebag said, "Why did the scientist disconnect his doorbell?"

"Why did he?"

"Because he wanted to win the Nobel Prize."

This broke up the Mexican blonde, and Shoebag giggled along with her in a hysterical, panic-stricken way.

"More! More!" cried the tarantula. "And when you can't think of anymore, it will be dinnertime."

Thirty-four

"How amusing! A Butterfinger!" said Mrs. Pedro Jiminez. "A snake, a frog, and a Butterfinger!"

"There *was* a spider here, once," said Miss Rattray.

"I guess it turned into a candy bar!" said the general, who was out of uniform now, but still very much an Army general. His voice boomed through the Science Room. "Someone is a magician. Is it *you*, Mr. Longo?"

Mr. Longo was red-faced and angry, hiding it with a sickly smile. "I am not known to be a magician," he said.

"We *needed* some comic relief," Ethel Lampert's mother spoke up. "The assembly speaker told me more than I wanted to know about how hard an actor's life is!"

"I'm glad my daughter heard that," said the general. "She is very involved with theater. She puts on her own plays, which she writes herself. It is not a good ambition to have if you want to get somewhere in this world!"

"My daughter," said Mrs. Lampert, "belongs to a secret club."

"The Betters?" Mrs. Jiminez asked.

"Not the Betters!" Mrs. Flower answered before Mrs. Lampert could. "*My* daughter is a Better, and she has never mentioned your daughter."

"My daughter says her club is better than the Betters," said Mrs. Lampert.

"Nothing is better than the Betters!" said Mrs. Jiminez. "The Betters did not want my poor daughter and it broke her heart!"

Miss Rattray intervened. "Well, now, we have seen the prizewinners, so let us move along out of here."

"But *where* is my daughter's spider?" Mrs. Flower asked, and she called over her shoulder, "C. Cynthia Ann! Where is your prizewinner?"

"I think it escaped," said Stanley Sweetsong.

Someone had to answer Mrs. Flower. Her daughter was too taken with Gregor Samsa to care where her spider was. She stood at the back of the Science Room looking up at the spokesboy, while he beamed down at her.

"The Mexican blonde didn't escape!" said Mr. Longo. "Someone took her! Someone put that Butterfinger there in her place."

"If you ask me," said Mrs. Lampert, "someone has a delightful sense of humor! I am so pleased I almost feel like making a contribution to this school!"

"*Almost?*" the quick-eared Miss Rattray said. "Why almost?"

"Well, I wouldn't want my money to go to more tanks for this room, unless," and she giggled at the thought, "they were for more Butterfinger tanks."

"*Moi aussi*," said Mrs. Flower, from whom C. Cynthia Ann had gotten her habit of slipping into French. "I would not want my beautiful daughter poring through more bug catalogs. She should be interested in important things like clothes and cosmetics. Not spiders, not my beautiful daughter!"

"Money is always needed," said Miss Rattray wisely, "and its use is not necessarily restricted to acquiring more tanks for this room."

Mrs. Lampert said, "I wish there were *no* tanks in this room. When I was a girl, we did not catch wild creatures and keep them locked in our schoolroom."

"But this is now their home, Mrs. Lampert," Miss Rattray said sweetly.

"They'd be better off in a zoo, Miss Rattray. Mr. Lampert and I contribute regularly to some excellent zoos."

Miss Rattray's ears perked up at the verb "contribute." "All things are possible," said she.

"But what *happened* to the Mexican blonde?" Mr. Longo said. "She was a very valuable spider."

C. Cynthia Ann Flower couldn't have cared less, anymore, about her expensive prizewinner.

She hooked her dainty little arm in Gregor Samsa's long arm and said, "Let me show you the rest of the school."

Miss Rattray nudged Stanley. "*You're* his escort, dear. You are the one to show him the rest of the school."

But when they looked behind them, Gregor and C. Cynthia Ann had disappeared.

The general said, "It seems the lovebirds have flown the coop, too."

Thirty-five

Butter, sleeping right under Stanley Sweetsong's desk, drawn by the strong scent of the tarantula, but fearful of her, too, opened one eye.

Cats do not like the sound of cockroach laughter.

Arachnid laughter was bad enough, and rare at that, but something about a roach giggle got on Butter's nerves.

And something about a particular roach roaming around the premises puzzled Butter, for not only could he change into a human when it suited him, apparently he could rise from the dead, as well.

Or was this another roach up there in the plastic container?

Butter opened both eyes.

More laughter . . . and Butter was off his rump and in a crouch, creeping carefully toward the desk.

A leap, and he was right next to the plastic container.

There was Cook's T-shirt with the faces of that old rock group on it!

Butter peered into the tank and saw the Mexican blonde stiffen as he brought up one paw, resting it on the piece of screen. Carefully, while the hairy spider dived behind the rock, Butter reached in. He fished the roach out and flipped him to the floor.

It was the same roach, all right, and Butter decided he should investigate him. Bite away the silk strings around his body. Maybe even taste him.

But a cat's playfulness always comes before his curiosity, and now that Butter knew the creature was not dead, but only playing dead, Butter would bat him around a bit.

He pushed the screen back in place, for Butter was wary of the tarantula, wary of all those tanksters from the Science Room.

Butter jumped down, ready for a little hockey game, using his paw for a stick and the wrapped-up roach for a puck.

Cats could always find fun games to play.

Thirty-six

With one long hand, its pointed nails beautifully manicured at the end of its long fingers, Miss Rattray plucked Stanley Sweetsong out of the procession leaving the Science Room.

"Don't think I don't know who put that Butterfinger in the tarantula's tank!" she said.

"Why would I do such a thing, ma'am?" said Stanley.

"*Butter*finger, *Butter* Club," Miss Rattray answered. "I am not all that dense that I cannot make that connection, Sweetsong."

"But only club members have keys to the Science Room, Miss Rattray."

"And *you* never will have a key to that room, at the rate you're going!" she told him.

Behind her, the general was waving his checkbook. "Miss Rattray? Let me leave something for you in my daughter's name. We are off to Tennessee momentarily, but we are in a good mood . . . and all we need is a pen."

"I have a pen," Stanley said, reaching into his pocket.

"Don't put it away after the general uses it," Ethel Lampert's mother called out. "I think I'll make a small contribution myself. Ethel has never seemed happier. Is that secret club she belongs to a stamp club?"

"If it is a secret club," Miss Rattray said, thinking fast, "probably its aims are secret, too."

Under her breath, Miss Rattray told Stanley, "We have a lot to talk about, Sweetsong, and —"

Now Mrs. Flower interrupted, "I have an extra pen, Miss Rattray, and Mrs. Lampert can use it *aprés moi*. For I intend to write a check myself, *providing* my daughter is discouraged from hunting down creatures for those unpleasant tanks!"

"And providing these poor unfortunates in the tanks get good homes in a proper zoo!" Mrs. Lampert called out.

Seldom so flustered she could be sidetracked from a scolding, Miss Rattray did not finish her remarks to Stanley. Instead, she called out, "Check-writers may follow me to my office where there are ample pens . . . and also chairs to sit on."

Then she turned back to Stanley. "You had better find Mr. Samsa, Sweetsong! After all, you *are* his escort."

"Yes, ma'am."

"Lucky for you," she said, "that this day did not

end in disaster. . . . Lucky for you that it had its benefits."

"Lucky for the snake and the frog, too," said Stanley.

"Lucky for Miss Rattray's School for Girls," Miss Rattray said, and sniffing, added, "and now . . . one boy."

Thirty-seven

So that was an actor!

Josephine Jiminez sat in the Music Room where she had reigned as P and thought about Gregor Samsa.

She was not eager to join the crowd flocking after him en route to the Science Room. She was too nervous to witness the Butter Surprise, for as P she would be responsible if anything went wrong.

No one had really understood Gregor Samsa's speech.

All the other speakers on Career Day had tried to make their jobs sound fascinating, but Samsa had shouted out "If you can give up theater, do it! Fast! Whatever you can give up, give it up! For it's only what you can't give up that will always work for you! Whether it's playing a bass fiddle, writing a play, loving someone, or studying to be a marine biologist, if you can't give it up, you will just have to do it!"

During the question period, someone had asked

him what he thought he would be, if he were not a star.

"A roach!" he'd answered. "A cockroach!"

There were gasps from the parents and giggles from the girls, and Miss Rattray had risen from her chair behind him on the podium and said, "Enough!" in the tone she used whenever she feared something was not going as planned.

Then as they'd all filed out of the auditorium, Josephine's mother had said to her, "Gregor Samsa seems to think as you do, dear: that if you're not important, you're like a roach."

"Gregor Samsa thinks like Dr. Dingle," Josephine answered. But there was no point, anymore, in trying to explain that misunderstanding. Nothing Josephine could say would change anything now.

After she took one last, long, loving look around the Music Room, Josephine sighed and set off to finish her packing.

As she walked back to her room, for the last time wearing her secret yellow sock under her regulation white one, her yellow WE'RE BUTTER badge pinned behind the lapel of her royal blue blazer, an opening line popped into her head.

It was Monroe talking. Act I. Scene I.

MONROE: "Bagg is your name? *Bagg?*"

He was addressing the googly-eyed doll, Huntsville, one of the Cast of Characters who rarely spoke.

HUNTSVILLE: Yes, Stuart Bagg. Here for the magical crowning of the Q of T."

MONROE: The Q of T? T has no Q!

Josephine decided she would call this new creation,

"Magic Can Happen Anywhere — Even In Tennessee."

She felt a slight lift to her walk as she climbed the stairs to the Lower School, and headed down the hall to her room. She was still concentrating on the play-in-progress for the Black Mask Theater when she came upon Butter, booting something about with one paw.

"What are you up to, Butter?"

The cat stopped, paw raised, eyes blinking.

Josephine bent down to see what it was.

The antennae were the only things the roach could move, for he was wrapped up like something left there by a spider.

"Give it up, Butter!" said Josephine. But remembering Gregor Samsa's assembly speech, and knowing a cat could not abandon such a grand game, Josephine picked the roach up herself.

No sooner had she done that than who should appear from around the corner?

"A cat!" shouted Gregor Samsa. "Oh, no!"

"It's only the kitchen cat," said C. Cynthia Ann Flower. "It's only Josephine Jiminez and the kitchen cat!"

Quickly, Gregor Samsa darted into Stanley Sweetsong's room. "Oh, no!" he shouted again. "The roach is gone! The roach must have been eaten alive!"

"What is all this about roaches?" said C. Cynthia Ann Flower, testily.

"Oh, no. Oh, no!" cried the Great Breath spokesboy returning to the hall, holding his head with both hands. "The roach has been eaten alive!"

"Who *cares* about roaches?" C. Cynthia Ann Flower said.

"Roaches have been around for two hundred-fifty million years!" said Gregor Samsa. "Now one of them is dead."

"*Not,*" Josephine Jiminez said.

"*Not?*" Gregor Samsa said.

"Look," Josephine Jiminez said.

She opened her hand with the roach in her palm.

"Eeeeek!" C. Cynthia Ann Flower screeched.

"Hooray!" said Gregor Samsa. "May I have him?"

"Don't hurt him," Josephine Jiminez said.

"Don't *touch* him!" C. Cynthia Ann Flower said.

But Gregor Samsa picked him up very gently.

"Put it down and step on it!" said C. Cynthia Ann.

"I don't step on things," Gregor Samsa said.

"I don't step on things, either," Josephine Jiminez told him.

"Now, let's get this little guy undone," said Gregor Samsa. "C. Cynthia Ann? You go on without me."

"Will you write me?" she asked him.

"Not if you step on things," he answered.

"I won't. I never will again!"

"She will so," said Josephine Jiminez.

"Only if it's *you,*" said C. Cynthia Ann.

The famous spokesboy was not listening to the girls. He was holding the roach very close to his long, thin face, and he was singing to him. Some strange little song about parties in kitchens.

Definitely a weirdo, Josephine Jiminez decided.

C. Cynthia Ann Flower had her limits: *Mon Dieu!*

Singing to a cockroach only proved Gregor Samsa's point, made that afternoon in assembly.

If you can give it up, do.

She did.

She fled, head held high as Miss Rattray's, feet moving as fast as Butter's, who trotted beside her. Red Better sock in place. WE'RE BETTER button pinned on.

She had better things to do than listen to a boy sing to a cockroach . . . and better boys in her future than the spokesboy for a chewing gum, which Miss Rattray's girls never chewed anyway.

Thirty-eight

I'd *love to chew Great Breath with you! Gregor Samsa.*

"Do you want it, Stanley?" Josephine Jiminez asked.

"He signed it for *you*," said Stanley, who didn't really want an autographed photograph of the Great Breath spokesboy.

"Gregor was nice," she said. "Weird but kind."

"Kind of weird."

"Stars aren't ever normal." Josephine flinched after she said the word "normal," so used to being sprayed by Dr. Dingle's sneeze. "So maybe *I* have a chance to be a star myself, someday, of something."

"Someday," Stanley agreed. "Of something."

They shifted around and looked away from each other.

"Well," said Stanley, "you'll be leaving now, hmmm?"

"Yes, off to the magic of Knoxville (known for

141

coal, marble, aluminum sheeting, and textiles), Tennessee." Josephine made a face.

Usually Stanley would grin at one of her cynical remarks, but smiling did not come easily at that moment.

It was hard to say good-bye.

"I really like your secret tarantularium," she said. "The Mexican blonde should be very happy in there."

"She'll be going to Castle Sweet in a week to live with Weezer."

"Will you tell all the Butters good-bye for me?"

"We'll remember our P every time we meet. We'll eat a Butterfinger in your memory."

"Step on C. Cynthia Ann Flower's toe once a month in assembly, in my memory," said Josephine.

"I will. It's the only thing I'll ever step on."

"And if you ever see Stuart Bagg again, tell him I'll get over it, and I'll get on with it."

"Hold your horses," Stanley said, reaching for the Hootie & The Blowfish T-shirt.

"That's what Bagg always said."

"I want you to take this."

"And that's his lucky T-shirt, Stanley."

"He never wanted to wear it, though. He liked my clothes better." He handed it to her and she thrust it into her bag, along with Monroe and the photograph of Gregor.

"Well . . . ahoy!" she said, her voice breaking.

"Ahoy and good-bye," said Stanley.

Then they shook hands in the secret way, thumbs-up and touching.

"We're Butter," they said together.

Thirty-nine

If ever someone saves your life, you should look out for whoever it is.

Stay near her.

Stick by her.

Shoebag knew that was what he had to do.

If ever you can find your way home, you should try to do it.

If you have a family somewhere you should try to find them.

Even if they live in Tennessee.

Even if they live inside a Macintosh.

Shoebag knew that was what he had to do.

Curled up in the ear of Monroe, the Kewpie doll, covered by the Hootie & The Blowfish T-shirt, he stared at the photograph of his good friend, Gregor Samsa.

"Before you ever try the formula again," Samsa had said, "be sure you have a good reason, and be sure to do it on a Wednesday night."

"But will it work? What if when I'm human I suddenly become a roach again?"

"Then you will have a lot of explaining to do," said Gregor, "which is why I'm glad I know *my* place."

It was dark inside the bag, but not bumpy any longer since Josephine had set it down on the floor, in the back seat of the Chrysler.

There were plenty of delicious crumbs scattered about near her comb and her change purse. Butterfinger crumbs, Pepperidge Farm goldfish crumbs, crumbs from Dipsy Doodles and Nabisco Old Fashioned Ginger Snaps . . . Shoebag would not go hungry.

It was the first time he had ever gone on a journey all by himself. Roachdom being what it was, he supposed it would not be the last time.

But for now: so long.

So long to Stanley Sweetsong and his Gap/ Levi's/Polo/Lands' End/Doc Marten wardrobe. Stanley would be okay from now on, Shoebag was sure.

So long to crabby Cook and crafty Butter.

So long to the jumping spider, Blonde, and the Zap man.

So long to Mr. Longo, the king snake, and the African frog.

So long to all the Butters, and even the Betters.

So long to Miss Rattray's School for Girls (and now one boy).

So long.

So long.

Until we meet again.